a window to the divine

CREATION THEOLOGY

ZACHARY HAYES, O.F.M.

ANSELM ACADEMIC

The publishing team included Jerry Ruff, general editor; prepress and manufacturing coordinated by the production departments of Anselm Academic.

Cover image royalty free from Shutterstock

First published in 1997 by Franciscan Press

Printed in the United States of America

7022

978-1-59982-018-7

Library of Congress Cataloging-in-Publication Data

Hayes, Zachary.
    A window to the divine : a study of Christian creation theology / by Zachary Hayes.
    p. cm.
Previously published: Franciscan Press, 1997.
Includes bibliographical references and index.
    ISBN 978-1-59982-018-7 (pbk.)
    1. Creation—History of doctrines. I. Title.
    BT695.H33 2009
    231.7'65—dc22

                                                                2008047283

Contents

Foreword

It is an honor to write a foreword for this publication of *A Window to the Divine*, authored by Fr. Zachary Hayes, OFM, a fellow Franciscan and former faculty colleague. First published in 1980, this introduction to the theology of creation became a standard reference in theology courses across North America for a decade and a half, until it went out of print. Revised, updated, and reissued in 1997, it again made its way onto the reading lists of courses dealing with the theology of creation where it still can be found. Under the imprint of Anselm Academic, it is now being made available for the third time, clearly a testimony to the enduring value it offers those engaged in the study of theology.

Father Hayes is widely knowledgeable in both theology and the sciences; he has been a long-time presenter and panelist for an interdisciplinary graduate seminar on the topic of creation. Readers will quickly discover the author's deep conviction threaded throughout this book. Science and religion, he insists, are truly able to enter into fruitful dialogue; they are not doomed to be adversaries. That dialogue requires a critical reading of both biblical texts and traditional teachings, to discern the theological vision embedded in the language and thought patterns of their time. It requires an openness to the scientific vision of the world advancing so rapidly today and in such amazing ways. (Think only of the spate of programs and publications on the history of planet earth and on the human genome project, on ecology and the future of our planet.) It requires a willingness to search for ways to express the theological vision of Scripture and Christian tradition in the language of today's scientific vision of the world.

The author's passion to integrate the worlds of religion and science, inherited from his own teachers and faithful to traditional Franciscan appreciation of theology and science, is woven into the fabric of his chapters on creation and human origins, on original sin, on creation and the future completion of the world. From his own Franciscan tradition, he also brings to these topics a vision of the central role of Christ in relation to creation, a cosmic Christology. Father Hayes makes only a modest claim for his book—he simply aims to sketch the outlines of a synthesis that might now be possible in light of the advances both in biblical-theological studies and in what science is now discovering about the world in which we live. He does not offer concrete solutions to the concerns being voiced ever more frequently and forcefully about a threatened ecology and the sustainability of life on planet earth. What he does offer is a framework, a theological vision that can anchor us as we seek ways to address these concerns, to give voice and witness to a Christian vision of the world in words that speak to people today. My fond hope is that readers will catch some of the author's passion to see, in an image he draws from Saint Bonaventure, that the world is a window to the divine.

Gilbert Ostdiek, OFM
Catholic Theological Union
Feast of St. Bonaventure

Preface

Questions related to creation theology were the object of considerable study and research in the 1950s and early 1960s. Individual problems were subjected to extensive study, and many valid insights were gained. A number of provocative studies suggested the shape that a general recasting of creation theology might take. Things seemed well on the way to a significant reformulation. However, with the close of the Second Vatican Council, most theological effort was understandably focused on the doctrine of the Church, which had played such an important role in the council. Then in the late 1960s and early 1970s, theological concern shifted to the problem of God in response to the growing sense of secularity and the appearance of various forms of the death-of-God theology. Subsequently the state of biblical studies and work on the history of doctrine brought about a shift in the area of Christology. It is in this area that the most creative work is being done now.

As a result, the development of creation theology was aborted in the early 1960s. In the meantime, the experience of environmental problems has served only to underscore the need for a solid, contemporary theology of creation; for it is in this area that theology can offer some significant insights to help define the relation of humanity to the physical world in which it is situated in the light of the wisdom of a major religious tradition.

This recent history of shifting theological concerns might help to explain why a sort of black hole exists in the area of contemporary studies on creation theology in the years following the council. Yet there is good reason to present a statement of the significant steps that have been taken in creation theology and to make them available to a wider audience. Our intention is to present a summary of developments on a number of basic questions pertaining to creation theology. This will be followed by the barest sketch of what a synthesis might look like at the present time. It is here above all that my personal roots in the tradition of Franciscan theology become obvious. I believe that this tradition contains a number of precious insights that can be developed to enrich the consciousness of the Church today.

Before taking up the questions that form the body of our presentation, we will point out two of the most basic factors that seem to undergird what may otherwise appear as a bewildering multiplicity of questions and problems. The first is a matter of methodology; the second is a matter of theological content.

The most significant changes in modern theology are at the level of methodology, for methodology determines how we approach theological content. If this is true of theology in general, it is clearly the case in the area of creation theology. The most significant change of method has to do with how we go about reading the texts of the tradition.

Most would agree that we should read these texts intelligently. But opinions may differ as to what constitutes an intelligent reading. The immense amount of work done on all levels, from the scientific to the popular, has familiarized many with the idea of approaching Scripture with some form of historical-critical method. Whatever one believes concerning inspiration, the fact remains that the actual texts of the Bible are human writings that have a long, complicated history. Though the idea of the historical-critical method has become familiar enough, it takes considerable time for the theological implications to emerge. This can be seen in the evaluation of the text of Genesis, chapter 13, which has played a pivotal role in the Church's doctrine of creation, anthropology, and sin over many centuries. Contemporary theology differs from our more familiar theology in terms of the instruments by which it attempts to unlock the meaning of the Bible.

Although historical-critical methods have become familiar in the context of Scripture, the application of similar methods to the texts of the councils and later theological works have been slower in arriving. We are seeing the impact of the historical-critical method more and more in recent years. It is the principal issue in reading the great Scholastic theology of creation in its religious, metaphysical, and physical dimensions. Likewise, it is the primary problem in reading the canons of the Council of Trent on original sin. If we keep in mind that the theologians treated in this book quite commonly share the conviction that the intelligent way of reading these texts involves not a simple repetition of the verbal formulas of the past but an attempt to determine what their authors intended to communicate with these formulas and to interpret the intended meaning for the vastly changed situation of the contemporary world, the major change in the new theological thought patterns will become clearer.

Concerning the shift in theological content, a quick glance at our familiar catechetical material will show that the doctrine of creation was presented for years with no reference to Christ. There are historical reasons for this, but it would take us too far afield to go into them. The extensive reading of both the Bible and the later tradition provides serious grounds for arguing that a specifically Christian theological understanding of creation must view the creation of the world in terms of its relation to Christ. Those familiar with the systems of Bonaventure and John Duns Scotus will readily recognize this as deriving from the medieval Franciscan tradition. Not only is Christ the revelation of God but also the revelation of the meaning of humanity and of the cosmos as well. Many theologians today are convinced that this traditional belief can be of great significance for theology as it attempts to address itself to the environmental issues that plague human society now.

The same Christocentric view of reality plays a significant role in some recent reformulations of the doctrine of sin. To speak of sin is to speak of a deficiency. But we cannot speak of a deficiency without assuming some norm or ideal. Since the norm of what humanity is called to become is embodied in Christ, the meaning of sin is seen in terms of our relation to Christ. This also comes from the tradition and is appropriated in a new way through efforts to deal with evolutionary thought patterns.

Because there is a great need for some sort of synthesis, I close my treatment with a sketchy description of what such a synthesis might look like if it were to be worked out in terms of the modern experience of the historicity of the world and of the human race. Such a sketch must leave many questions untouched. At most, it can hope to describe the framework within which particular questions must be treated. In my opinion, the suggestions for such a synthesis are solidly rooted in the tradition of theology and reflect the conviction that the deeper religious concerns of the tradition remain valid concerns for humanity in the complex world of the twentieth century. The significance of such concerns will become clear only if we can say that fidelity to a tradition does not require that the Christian be an antiquarian who denies the basic qualities of the modern experience of the world and of ourselves as human beings within the world.

If we read the work of the great Saint Augustine, it will become obvious that in his view, the entire cosmos is a vast symbolic language system the content of which is the eternal, divine Word. Using another sort of metaphor, he refers to the universe as a *carmen Dei*—a song of God, and he is profoundly impressed by the *splendor ordinis*—the splendor of order—to be discovered in the world of creation. Centuries later, the great medieval theologian and mystic Saint Bonaventure compared the world of creation to a splendid stained-glass window. The light of divine truth, goodness, and beauty is refracted through the fabric of the universe as physical light is refracted in a rich fabric of shapes and colors by the windows of the great Gothic cathedrals under construction even as Bonaventure wrote. Or again, for Bonaventure as for Augustine, the world may be seen as a book containing the very revelation of the mystery of God. The problem for many, he mused, is that the glorious book of the universe had become virtually illegible. It had become like a foreign language. The meaning of this primal book of divine revelation in nature needed to be opened by another book; that book is "written within and without" in the mystery of Jesus Christ, the incarnate Word of God through whom all things are created and brought to completion.

Today the insights of the sciences have opened our minds to a cosmos immensely vaster in space and time than anyone before the modern period of history could have imagined. Many today feel that the *carmen Dei* of which Augustine spoke may be more like a Mahler symphony in complexity, density, and extent. With an eye on the vision of our past, one is tempted to ask whether it is still possible for believers who are literate in the modern sciences to hear a divinely inspired song or symphony, or whether the mysterious universe held out to us by the work of the sciences can still be seen, in Bonaventure's terms, as a window to the divine.

This book springs from the conviction that it is indeed possible for contemporary believers to sense a remarkably rich communication of the divine mystery precisely through the insights of the sciences. For those with a sense of the depth and richness of the Christian tradition, there is no reason to assume that there must be an adversarial relationship between faith and science. There is every reason, on the other hand, to expect that the exciting insights of the sciences may open even richer and more challenging possibilities to the understanding of our tradition. Our tradition is rooted in the belief that however the universe may look empirically, it is precisely this universe described to us at the empirical level by the sciences that our faith holds to be the fruit of God's creative knowledge and love. It is my hope that these reflections may help us discover in what sense this universe may truly be seen as a window to the mystery of the divine.

– 1 –

Science and Theology

Recent History of the Question

The doctrinal treatment of creation has long been the area in which Christians have most emphatically posed the question of the relation between science and theology. This is particularly clear in modern times because of the apparent conflicts between the long-familiar worldview reflected in the ordinary presentation of the theology of creation on the one hand and the gradually emerging new worldview implied in the post-Renaissance sciences on the other hand. The threat of disorientation stemming from the collapse of a worldview was eloquently expressed as early as the seventeenth century in the poetry of John Donne, who wrote in reference to the views of Copernicus and Galileo:

> And new Philosophy calls all in doubt,
> The Element of fire is quite put out;
> The Sun is lost, and th' earth, and no man's wit
> Can well direct him, where to looke for it. . . .
> 'Tis all in pieces, all cohearance gone;
> All just supply, and all Relation. . . .
> For the world's beauty is decayed, or gone,
> Beauty, that's color, and proportion.[1]

---

1 *The Complete Poetry of John Donne*, ed. J. T. Shawcross, with introduction, notes, and variants. The Anchor-Seventeenth Century series (NY, 1967) pp. 271–286, esp. pp. 277–278.

That the problem of the relation between science and theology should be posed so clearly in the question of creation is not surprising if the matter is viewed with an eye to the broader tradition of Western Christian theology. Two of the major concerns of theology traditionally have been (1) to provide a relatively coherent understanding of faith for the community of believers, and (2) to mediate religious meaning and values to the culture at large. In as far as the experience of the believers is deeply conditioned by the categories of the culture in which they live, the implementation of both tasks is possible only to the degree that the world of faith is willing to speak in terms of the world of meaning present in the culture. Thus, at some level, theology must take up the task of speaking about faith issues in terms of the concrete world of ordinary and scientific experience in a given cultural situation. It is largely, though not exclusively, in the area of creation theology that this has been done. In the past, the willingness to take up this task has led to the creation of theologies that incorporated elements of the Platonic or the Aristotelian worldview into the very fabric of theology. That form of theology most familiar to Christians of the twentieth century is the style created by the Scholastic incorporation of Aristotelian physics and metaphysics as structural elements of Christian theology.

The awareness of these Aristotelian influences on Christian theology sheds light on the history of the attempts to deal with science and theology in recent times. If scientific or prescientific views of the world enter into the structure of a theology in some way, and if believers forget where a style of theology has come from and what elements have entered into its structure, what would one expect to happen when the scientific vision of the world begins to change?

Though this is certainly not the only factor in the famous Galileo case, it is certainly a major concern in understanding what happened in this instance.[2] The major theological vision of reality received from the medieval theologians reflected a geocentric vision of the physical universe. The change suggested by Copernicus and Galileo from a geocentric to a heliocentric view was a challenge to the entire worldview in which theology had been constructed. This

---

2 See J. J. Langford, *Galileo, Science, and the Church* (NY, 1966) for a competent treatment of this complex case.

is precisely what the poem of John Donne refers to. Just as Aristotle had appeared to threaten the familiar theology of the early Scholastics, so the unfamiliar world suggested by Galileo appeared to threaten the familiar theology of the sixteenth and seventeenth centuries with its Aristotelian underpinnings. It is understandable that the new scientific view would appear as the enemy. One of the significant effects of the Galileo case may be seen in the separation between science and theology. Effective dialogue became impossible, and theology continued its work in the familiar categories of the late Middle Ages while science went on its own way independently of any theological concern.

The sciences continued to develop. In the nineteenth century, Darwin's theory of evolution raised questions concerning the origin of the human race and the extent of human history. Again a scientific theory appeared as the opponent of long-familiar theological views. In the twentieth century, the development of atomic physics and astrophysics has led us to a worldview that seems foreign not only to the world of theology but also to the world of commonsensical experience. Indeterminism (Heisenberg) and the relativity theory (Einstein) have changed our experience of the world profoundly. The vision of an expanding universe characterized by the qualities reflected in the realm of chaos theory and complexification theory have created a vision of the cosmos unprecedented in human history. The immensity of the universe in terms of space and time has become familiar to anyone who has received even minimal exposure to courses in science and has become grist for the mill of science fiction in literature as well as in movies and television.

The world of science has developed with giant strides. Some say that the modern world is standing on the brink of a new cosmology. Be that as it may, the worldview mediated to both believer and unbeliever alike by our modern culture is radically different from that which provided some key structural elements for our familiar theological vision and language. Though it is not possible at the present to speak of a universally accepted scientific vision of the universe, a number of basic concerns can be singled out.

First, the question of the relation between science and theology is not simply the question of whether Christians may accept the theory of biological evolution. It is a much more fundamental question than that. It is the question of the possibility of theologizing in reference to a fundamentally changed worldview within which the question of biological evolution is only one question among many. Second, while we cannot speak of a universally accepted scientific view, it is possible to single out some specific elements commonly present in the contemporary mood. In a basic sense, there has been a shift from a finished and stable universe to a universe in constant change and flux. Whereas our familiar theology, following Parmenides and Aristotle, placed primary emphasis on stability and situated change within a metaphysics of being, the modern experience is more akin to that of Heraclitus, placing primary emphasis on change and treating stability within a metaphysics of becoming. In essence, this reflects a deep sense of the historicity of the world and of humanity that must be dealt with in a Christian theology, above all in the theology of creation.

Science has continued to develop, and its vision is mediated to us culturally in many ways. But what has happened to the world of theology? By and large, the reaction of modern theology has been considerably less courageous than was that of Aquinas in the thirteenth century. We can distinguish a number of stages of reaction. Beginning with the Galileo case, we can speak of a relation of open warfare between science and theology. While many of the great names among the scientists were believers in their personal lives, still for many simple believers as well as for many theologians, science was the enemy, and the task of theology was to prove the enemy wrong. A similar type of reaction to Darwin is reflected in the abundant antievolutionary literature of the late nineteenth and early twentieth centuries.[3] Generally, today such open hostility has cooled off and remains only in the cases of religious fundamentalism or in an uncritical approach to the sciences.

The nineteenth century saw the emergence of certain forms of concordism that sought to create more positive relations between what had been seen as warring parties. Concordism reflected the conviction that either certain claims of theology could be proven by science, or that the limitations of scientific knowledge could be filled out with information from the world of religion. Thus, as an example,

---

3 See E. Ruffini, *The Theory of Evolution Judged by Reason and Faith* (NY, 1959).

it was hoped that the historicity of the Flood could be proven by geological evidence. Or, as another example, once it was recognized that the Hebrew word for *day* does not necessarily refer to a period of twenty-four hours but can mean an indefinite period of time, the six days of creation in Genesis might possibly coincide with geological ages in the history of our planet. For various reasons, concordism was found wanting, and one scarcely finds it around today except in certain forms of biblical fundamentalism.

We enter the twenty-first century with an unresolved question. Not only is it unresolved, but a number of new factors enter into the picture. A new cultural factor can be seen in the emergence of various forms of existential and personalist philosophy in Europe between the two world wars. A new theological factor is the neo-orthodox reaction to Protestant liberalism, a reaction initiated largely by Karl Barth. The combination of these two factors has led to a variety of positions reflecting the conviction that science and theology are two unrelated disciplines and ought to remain such. Since they deal with such fundamentally different concerns, there can be neither conflict nor mutual support. Theology will be largely existential in tone, and the doctrine of creation will be seen as having no bearing on our understanding of the physical world that is the concern of science.

While such an existential style has much to commend itself, it is felt by many to be inadequate since it removes from theology the most obvious point of contact with the important ideas that shape modern consciousness. Theologians as well as critical scientists have become increasingly aware that such an approach does not solve the basic questions but merely bypasses them. Such a radical separation between science and theology fails to take into account the cognitive claims of the Christian religious tradition. Furthermore, it provides no framework for discussing the relation between God and the processes of the world of nature.

Some of the basic philosophical assumptions operative in the theoretical understanding of the sciences have been subjected to a significant critique by Michael Polanyi.[4] In his discussion of the extreme positivist understanding of science, Polanyi concentrates on the methodological separation of science and religion. Science, it was

---

4 Polanyi, *Personal Knowledge: Towards a Post-Critical Philosophy* (Chicago, 1958).

assumed, is a discipline of objectivity, whereas religion implies the personal involvement and commitment of the believer to the object of faith. Ideally, the scientist is the neutral, uninvolved observer of the facts and processes of the physical world. But the theologian, whose task it is to reflect on religion, is unavoidably enmeshed in the problems of involvement, commitment, and subjectivity. In response to this view, Polanyi demonstrates persuasively that the presumed objectivity of the scientist in fact reflects a good deal of personal involvement and commitment that had been seen as characteristic of the theologian. A complete dichotomy between involvement and objectivity does not exist; there are only varying degrees of involvement and commitment to the pursuit of truth in the two disciplines. Thus Polanyi and others like him give reason to reject any absolute dichotomy between science and theology at the most fundamental levels that concern the nature of method and epistemology.

Quite independently of Polanyi and his analysis, theologians operating largely from the centuries-long Roman Catholic tradition have attempted to create a theological vision, however tentative, that employs major insights from the modern, scientific worldview (Rahner, Hulsbosch, Schoonenberg, Pendergast). Their work reflects the inspiration of Teilhard de Chardin in varying degrees. A number of Protestant theologians have tended to make express use of the process philosophy of Whitehead and Hartshorne to create a theology with a distinctively modern shape (Cobb, Ogden, Overmann).

Pope John Paul II spoke on the question of the relation between science and faith on a number of occasions. He saw some form of conversation between the two as crucial for the future of life on this planet. Both, he argued, ought to be taken up in the common human enterprise of investing human life with meaning in the world as we now perceive it. He insisted on the autonomy of the two disciplines and did not look to some form of reduction of one to the other. The papal statements did not take up particular areas or themes of theology. On the contrary, they were largely programmatic in character and pointed to the importance of dialogue with the sciences as a direction for the future of theology.[5]

---

5 Z. Hayes, "God and Theology in an Age of Scientific Culture," in *New Theology Review* (August 1995) pp. 5–18.

Models for Relating Theology and Science

Thus, we arrive at the present with no universally accepted resolution to the question of the relation between science and theology. If the nature of theology is understood in a certain way, some findings of science appear to have a direct relevance for theology. Thus, in Roman Catholic circles, scientific views on the polygenetic origins of the human race are commonly understood to have a direct theological relevance, specifically with respect to the Church's doctrine concerning original sin. It is possible to speak also of an indirect relevance of science for theology. For example, recent attempts to define the relation between science and theology have contributed to a new understanding of some basic theological categories such as revelation and religious truth. It would be quite incomplete to try to account for these changes solely in terms of the internal development of biblical exegesis. This itself is part of the larger emergence of historical consciousness in which many other nontheological disciplines have played a significant role and have influenced theology at least indirectly. No convincing argument can be produced to demonstrate that science is in no way relevant to theology. On the contrary, the major Western theological tradition operates on assumptions that imply that science has some relevance for theology. The major attempts to formulate the relation between the two can be summarized in the following way.

Either there is no relation between them, or there is some relation that is difficult to define exactly. Those who hold that there is no relation may represent one of two basic positions. The first position tends to think that science and religious faith necessarily stand in an adversarial relation to each other. Thus, a religious believer may be convinced that the world of faith and theology simply possesses the truth, including much significant truth about the nature and history of the physical world. Theology, conceived in this way, has no real need of science. And if science should conflict with the world of theology in any way, it is clear that science is wrong. This view is characteristic of various forms of fundamentalism and of the so-called scientific creationism for which the Bible contains divinely revealed scientific information. Since this information is divinely inspired, it has the strongest possible legitimation. But then, on the contrary, a person who is thoroughly convinced of the importance and the adequacy of science may think that religion is hopelessly mired in ignorance and fear of reality. All one really needs to make one's way through life is the best knowledge that science can provide. All else is fantasy. From either perspective, religion and science are unavoidably enemies of each other.

A second position holds that theology and science have their own truths and their appropriate methods. The two are simply mutually exclusive realms of human thought and discourse. They can neither affirm nor contradict each other. They simply deal with different realities. Such an approach has the advantage of liberating theology from the constantly changing insights and theories of science even as it allows for the legitimacy of science in its own proper concerns. It has the disadvantage, however, of removing theology from effective communication with many of the important ideas that shape human life.

Aside from these two strongly polarized positions, there are those who, for a variety of reasons, are convinced that there ought to be some form of relation between theology and the sciences. But there is no unanimity as to precisely how one ought to define this relation. One can look to science to provide proofs for certain claims of religion, or one can look to revelation for the completion of our scientific knowledge of the world as in the case of concordism. Or one can adopt the view that recognizes the proper methodological autonomy of science and theology but holds that religious faith must express itself in relation to the secular categories by which human people give some shape to their world. Faith, one might argue, must be seen in relation to the way we perceive the world physically and conceive of it metaphysically; religion mediates its concerns and values through a theology that speaks in terms of a scientific and philosophical worldview. Therefore, we will not expect science to prove faith claims, nor will we expect theology to prove the claims of science. But we will attempt to allow religious faith to express itself in terms relevant to its cultural context, which, at least in the Western world of the present, is strongly conditioned by scientific insights.

By pursuing such an approach, we can eventually find some degree of coherence between faith and our secular cultural experience. And the values of faith can be mediated in an intelligible way to people deeply impressed by scientific culture. If such a policy were carried out, it might overcome the sort of spiritual schizophrenia so common in the modern believer; a state in which believers see the world through one pair of glasses religiously and through another pair in terms of the rest of their life experiences. It would be possible also to provide a framework for creative discussion between religion and culture. In principle, it would become possible to formulate a positive answer to the question as to whether the Christian religious ideal coincides in any way with the human ideal of responsibility for the world. Thus we could expect theology to say something significant concerning the problems raised by modern science and technology.

While such an approach does have many appealing qualities about it, unless theologians remain conscious of the inner dynamic of this thought process, it can also lead to the same sort of problems that were experienced in the Galileo case; a familiar scientific view of the world can become so closely identified with faith that any change will again appear as a threat to faith. Yet it is this model that best corresponds to the major Western Christian tradition as it was known before the Galileo case, and it offers the most fruitful possibility for Christianity in the modern Western world.

Questions of Origins

The history of this problem leads to the possibility of a more careful reading of the texts of the theological tradition concerning creation. What appear to the uncritical eye as straight-forward eyewitness descriptions of the creation of the world can be seen to involve various levels of questions which may be legitimately distinguished in interpreting the texts of the tradition. What at first seems to be a clear description of God's work in creating the world can be seen as a basically religious statement clothed in language and images drawn from scientific or pre-scientific images of the world, the latter serving as the vehicle of the former. The concrete image of the world is not to be taken as the content of the divine revelation but as the means whereby a religious insight is communicated.

In reading the texts of the theological tradition that bear specifically on the issue of creation, L. Gilkey distinguishes three types of questions that appear as questions of origin.[6]

---

6 *Maker of Heaven and Earth: The Christian Doctrine of Creation in the Light of Modern Knowledge* (Garden City, 1959, 1965 pbk.) pp. 15–40.

The first is the sort of question which is the concern of the physical sciences. Such questions are principally concerned with the causes in the world of nature; they enquire about those factors in a particular situation which bring about another situation. Briefly, they are questions of physical cause and effect in relation to our space-time experience. When the scientist asks about the origins of the universe, this is a question of tracing the chain of cause-effect as far back as possible and making conjectures concerning the original space-time situation. This is a legitimate sort of question about the concrete conditions that have brought us to where we find ourselves in the history of the cosmos. This is the type of question involved when we speak of the Big-Bang theory, the Nebular hypothesis, the Steady-State theory, etc. All of these theories are scientific attempts to provide a coherent account of the chain of cause and effect that has brought the universe to its present condition. Such questions correspond to what Scholastic theology called secondary causality. In Scholastic thought, secondary causality must be distinguished from primary causality, which is proper to God alone.

This sort of question must be distinguished from another kind that may be called the philosophical question of origins. The philosophical question is perhaps best understood in terms of that sort of primordial wonder at the fact that there is anything that exists at all. Why is there something rather than nothing? It can be seen immediately that this is a different sort of question altogether. In dealing with this type of question, philosophy will develop its own understanding of the fundamental structures of being; it will develop metaphysics in some form. Again, this is a legitimate sort of human question in response to the world in which we find ourselves. It is clearly distinct from the sort of scientific question referred to earlier. What counts as a significant answer to such a question will be judged by criteria different from those of the positive sciences.

While both the scientific question and the philosophical question can be seen as questions of origin, they are not to be confused with the religious question which, according to Gilkey, is first of all a question of existential meaning. It is the question of the meaning of human life. It seeks to determine how such meaning is ultimately grounded. What ultimately conditions my life? Why do I exist? What must I do with my life? What can I hope for in my life? In general, the religious question articulates itself eventually in the form of theology; and more specifically as a question of origins, it takes the form of the doctrine of creation.

Aware of these distinctions, we can see how these varied levels of concern are fused in the texts of the theological tradition. Failure to distinguish them will lead to inevitable confusion concerning modern science and philosophy. On the other hand, when these are recognized as legitimately distinct levels of question, the possibility of distinguishing the content from the form of the religious issue is opened up; and with this opening we are challenged further to the task of creatively interpreting that religions concern in a new scientific situation. Rather than fearing the ongoing discoveries of science, we can work with the conviction that scientific knowledge can enlarge and enrich not only our understanding of the world, but our view of God and of God's way of acting as well.

-2-

A New Reading
of the Sources

The theology of creation has traditionally appealed to certain texts of Scripture for its basis and has worked itself out historically in dialogue with a number of alternate positions concerning the origin of the world. Textual criticism has made a fresh reading of the scriptural sources both necessary and possible. A similar historical, critical method applied to later texts of the theological tradition opens up a new understanding of the later developments as well. Alerted by an analysis such as Gilkey's, we can now read the basic texts in such a way as to distinguish the various levels of concern present in them.

Scripture

Hebrew Scriptures

Familiar presentations of the theology of creation commonly appeal to the opening chapters of the book of Genesis as the basis for the Church's doctrine on creation. All too often, at least at the popular level, it happens that these texts are understood to be, to some degree, an eyewitness account of the beginning of the universe and of the human race. The factual character of these events becomes all-important for the understanding of the faith, since all seems to stand or fall with these alleged facts.

Such an interpretation of Genesis is of relatively recent origin and does not represent the much longer tradition of the Fathers and the Scholastics, who indeed accepted a literal, historical level of meaning as self-evident, but for whom the true religious meaning was found only at the level of spiritual interpretation.[1] As this level of interpretation is unfolded by means of allegory and other techniques, the descriptions of the beginning of history commonly become a structure for interpreting what is happening throughout the whole of history, both in the life of the individual and in the life of the human race as such. Sermons and commentaries on the creation accounts more often than not take the form of a theology of history that goes far beyond the understanding of Genesis as bald, historical accounts. Such an appeal to spiritual interpretation dominated Christian theology until it was gradually replaced by a one-dimensional understanding in various forms of fundamentalism that developed in the modern period by way of reaction to the growth of biblical criticism and the development of the modern positive sciences.

Recent historical, textual studies have led to the possibility of moving beyond this limited, positivistic approach to Scripture. It has become clear that the texts that now stand at the beginning of the Hebrew Scriptures do not represent the beginning of the literary history of the Bible.[2] They seem to be relatively late accounts of beginnings fashioned partly in light of Israel's experience of the Exodus and the Covenant of Sinai, and partly in light of the experience of the Davidic and Solomonic kingship. The present redaction of the material probably comes from the postexilic period of Jewish history.

Viewpoints among exegetes differ as to whether the earlier creation traditions were inserted into the later covenant tradition, or whether the covenant tradition was inserted into the creation tradition. Regardless of how this question might be resolved, the conjunction of the two traditions in the present form of the texts affects the identification of the saving God of the Covenant with the creator God of the world. The particular experience of the Hebrew people is seen within a universal context. What we now find at the beginning of the Bible may well be seen as a case of religious legitimation. That is, the experience of the presence of a saving God in the Covenant experience is grounded in the broadest possible way when

---

1 H. De Lubac, *The Sources of Revelation* (NY, 1968) pp. 11–72.
2 L. Scheffczyk, *Creation and Providence* (NY, 1970) pp. 4–20.

the God of this particular people is identified with the Lord of the world and of history. The God who saves is the God who creates. And this God creates not only Israel but all other peoples and the whole world in which human history is enacted.

Because of the elements drawn from the earlier tribal traditions, the first chapters of Genesis appear to reflect parallels with the cosmologies of other early Near Eastern religions, but because these traditions have been reshaped in the light of Israel's own religious experience, a closer examination reveals many fundamental differences.

One of the implications of the historical development of biblical texts is that though the creation accounts now stand at the beginning of our Bible, creation theology in its present form was not the literary starting point of the Hebrew Scriptures. One of the more influential attempts to formulate the theological significance of this is found in Karl Barth: "Creation is the outer ground of covenant; and covenant is the inner ground of creation."[3] This formulation emphasizes the religious understanding of creation theology rather than any form of physical cosmology. God creates for an end or purpose that becomes known in the history of the Hebrew people. God creates for the purpose of entering into covenant relations with humanity. The doctrine of creation emphasizes the universal dimensions of the religious experience of a particular people.

The process of appropriating the mythical, tribal traditions in light of later experiences has been described in detail by numerous exegetes.[4] From the viewpoint of the systematician, Rahner has highlighted the need for a proper means of interpreting the biblical texts in the light of their historical genesis and uses the term *historical etiology* to underscore what is really happening in the history of these texts.[5]

---

3   K. Barth, *Die Kirchliche Dogmatik*, III/1 (Zurich, 1957) pp. 103–258; *Mysterium Salutis: Grundriss heilsgeschichtlicher Dogmatik*, ed. J. Feiner, M. Löhrer, II (Einsiedeln, Zurich, Cologne, 1967) pp. 441–454.

4   H. Renckens, *Israel's Concept of the Beginning: The Theology of Genesis 1-3*. (NY, 1964); B. Anderson, *Creation versus Chaos: The Re-interpretation of Mythical Symbolism in the Bible* (NY, 1967); C. Westermann, *Creation*, tr. J. J. Scullion (Philadelphia, 1974).

5   K. Rahner, *Hominisation: The Evolutionary Origin of Man as a Theological Problem* (NY, 1965) pp. 36–44. This English text is the translation of Rahner's contribution to an earlier German work: K. Rahner & P. Overhage, *Das Problem der Hominisation* (Freiburg, 1958).

Conceived as an etiology, the texts represent an attempt to locate and give expression to the basic causes of the present experience of the people, which includes the experience of goodness and promise as well as the experience of sin and evil. The goodness and promise of life are grounded in the theological fact of origins from a good, loving God, whereas the experience of sin and evil is grounded in the historical mode in which human beings have responded to God.

Such an approach to the texts makes it possible to recognize the distinction between the deep theological significance of the texts of Genesis on one hand, and the mythical expression of this theological concern on the other hand. As often as the Hebrew Scriptures give expression to the religious vision involved in terms of the concrete world, this takes the form of the prescientific, mythical understanding available from the surrounding culture. Recognizing this distinction has the further effect of raising the challenge of expressing this religious concern in terms of a different concrete experience of the world. If the religious message is identified with the concrete imagery used to express it, modern science and the Bible are inevitably condemned to conflict. Recognizing the distinction as described here makes it possible to be fully serious about the religious concern and take up the challenge of expressing it in relation to the modern experience of the physical world.

It is clear, moreover, that the texts of Genesis are not the only texts of the Bible that speak of creation. In fact, if the present form of the Genesis texts is to be understood as coming from some form of backward projection, the reading of the prophetic literature indicates that the notion of creation is the object of a forward projection as well. In this case, the notion of creation points to the future when God will bring the divine work of creation to fulfillment. Thus, creation is related to the gradually emerging future consciousness of the Hebrew people, and eschatological fulfillment is spoken of as a "new creation" or a "re-creation."[6] More and more, the term *creation* refers not simply to something that God did "in the beginning," but to something God is engaged in throughout history. The whole of history is initiated by God, who is present always in it, and who will bring to a victorious completion what was initiated "in the beginning."

---

6 Ps. 102: 26–28; Jer. 31:22; 43:14–21; Is. 51:27ff; 65:17; 66:22.

Protology is intimately related to eschatology. Theology of creation is bound up with theology of history.

These remarks on the present reading of the Hebrew creation texts have been brief, but they indicate some of the more significant reasons why theologians today are inclined to see the doctrine of creation in the Hebrew Scriptures primarily as a religious confession rather than as a physical cosmology. It seems sufficiently clear that creation theology has a legitimating function in relation to covenant faith, which is a far more central religious category. Creation theology as it appears in the Hebrew Scriptures functions to ground salvation hopes in the real order. It is clear, furthermore, that the expression of this religious faith employs symbols, stories, and a physical cosmology that manifest clear parallels with the accounts of origins in the other religions of the ancient world, though these elements have been shaped and reformed by the confrontation with Israel's own religious experience.

The Christian Scriptures

If the movement in the Hebrew Scriptures is from the hope of salvation to the grounding of this hope in creation, a similar movement can be perceived in the Christian Scriptures. The major shift involved here is that Christians must now take the mystery of Christ into consideration. As the Hebrew experience of God's saving presence centered largely around the Covenant, so the Christian experience of salvation centered around the experience that "God was reconciling the world to himself in Christ" (2 Cor. 5:19). If creation theology in the Hebrew Scriptures appears largely as the condition for Covenant, so in the Christian Scriptures it will appear in a Christ-centered vision of God's relation to the world and to the human race.

This shift is not noticeably present in the Synoptic Gospels, which, for the most part, reflect the Jewish tradition of creation as the context for the preaching of the Kingdom in the ministry of Jesus. The Kingdom metaphor, which is basic to the preaching of Jesus, elicits an awareness of that goal that God intends "from the foundation of the world" (Mt. 25:34). It is particularly in Paul's letters and John's Gospel that this shift can be seen clearly. The special contribution of Paul rests in the conviction that God creates the world in

Christ.[7] The history of salvation, which is initiated by God's creative action, is ordered to the mystery of Christ, which in turn anticipates the destiny of the human race.

This understanding would provide the basis for a tradition of Christocentric creation theology in later centuries. In this style of theology, the Father appears as the source and goal of creation. Christ is the mediator of creation, salvation, and consummation. This possibility of a universal mediatorship is rooted in the theological notion of the preexistent Son, who is incarnate in Jesus of Nazareth. The fact that the person of the eternal Son is identical with the person of the incarnate Son provides the basis for affirming an inner, positive relation between the order of creation and the order of salvation through the one mediator. God creates for the sake of the final fulfillment accomplished in Christ.

O. Cullmann[8] notes that the prologue to the Gospel of John amounts to nothing less than a rewriting of the opening of the book of Genesis in light of the Christ mystery. In Jesus we are confronted with the eternal Word through whom God creates the world. He is the Word through whom God enlightens all who come into the world, bringing both light and life to those who receive him. He who has been operative in the world from the beginning now "sets up his tent" among us in the person of Jesus. The confluence of creation motifs and covenant motifs, and the mystery of Jesus Christ provide a strong impetus for affirming the fundamental unity of creation and salvation. Such a development may be seen to reflect the Christian conviction of the universal significance of the Christ event, which is seen to be decisive in the world and in its history. If this is the case, it can hardly have been inserted into history as an afterthought. Only when the line of salvation is rooted at the origin of the line of creation can the universality of salvation be seriously affirmed.

Not only is the mystery of creation interpreted in light of Christ, but the terminology of creation is used to express the effects of the Christ event in human life and ultimately in eschatology. The goal of God's creative action is not merely the fact of existence, but a quality

---

7   1 Cor. 8:6; Eph. 1:3–14; Col. 1:15–20.
8   *The Christology of the New Testament*, tr. S. Guthrie and C. Hall (Philadelphia, 1959) pp. 247–248, 262–269.

of life. The old order finds its goal in the quality of our life in Christ. Our historical share in the grace of salvation appears as a new, higher act of creation.[9] If the experience of the new creation is interpreted in the language of grace, then grace finds its fullest realization not in history but in eschatological fulfillment. What has happened in Christ is the anticipation of the collective future of the human race. The full realization of the new life in Christ will be found with Christ in the presence of the Father. Symbols of this in the Christian Scriptures are the Kingdom, the new heaven and the new earth, etc.

In this sense, the work of the first creation comes to its fulfillment in the eschatological renewal of reality in the saving presence of God. Such a reading of the Christian creation texts sees the mystery of creation not simply in terms of the beginnings of the physical universe, but preeminently in religious terms as the placing of the beginning of finite being that finds its consummation in the mystery of Christ and the eschatological dimension embodied in him. All flows from the creative action of God, which, more specifically, flows from the Father and is mediated through the Son. The history of the world and of the human race hold together in the person of Christ.

It seems fair to conclude that just as in the Hebrew Scriptures, the account of origins is not an eyewitness report of the physical beginnings of the world, but a faith-inspired grounding of the salvation hopes of the Hebrew people in the ground of the universe, so the Christian creation theology is the reflection on origins from the standpoint of the Christ event. Its purpose is not to provide information about events in the physical history of the cosmos, but to provide the widest legitimation of the Christian religious experience of the saving presence of God in Christ.

In summary, such a reading of the biblical sources clarifies that the doctrine of creation is not merely a question of interpreting the Genesis accounts at the beginning of the Bible. It is a question of reading and interpreting the many texts that speak of creation in terms of what seem to be clear facts in the historical development of the Bible. Viewed from this perspective, both the Hebrew and the Christian Scriptures reflect an actualistic understanding of creation

---

9 Rm. 5:12–21; 1 Cor. 15:45; Gal. 6:15; 2 Cor. 5:17; Rm. 6:4, Eph. 2:15; 4:24; Col. 3:10.

in which God's creative action is an abiding reality and is always the precondition for salvation. The doctrine of creation is primarily a religious confession, not a physical cosmology. Yet in relating this religious conviction to the world experience available at the time, the writers of the Bible make use of the then current prescientific physical worldview.

Comparing the Hebrew Scriptures with the Christian Scriptures, we can conclude that the view of creation in the Christian texts is reshaped significantly in view of the person of Christ. Both protology and eschatology for Christian theology are deeply conditioned by Christ, who functions as preexistent Son, as incarnate Son, and as glorified Lord. Since he is the principle of unity between creation, grace, and consummation, he is intrinsic to God's plan from the beginning.

In brief, the theology of creation in both the Hebrew and Christian Scriptures appears as a theology of history deeply tied to the gradually emerging future consciousness of the Jewish and the Christian communities. It is a theology that sees created being emerging from God's creative action in a temporal process that is ordered to a level of completion not possessed in history. In the Christian Scriptures, the decisive step to that consummation is realized in the mystery of Christ.

Brief though it is, this survey of the biblical theology of creation may serve to illustrate one of the major shifts of concern in the contemporary theology of creation. In a Christian theology of creation, we cannot fail to take into account the texts of the Christian Scriptures that at certain levels present the mystery of creation in deeply Christocentric terms. It becomes sufficiently clear that for a Christian theology of creation, regardless of how one may read the opening chapters of Genesis, it is not sufficient merely to recount the stories presented there.

Indeed, a history of biblical texts must be taken into account, and that history reaches a significant level for Christian theology precisely at the level of Christological reflection. According to these later levels of inspired reflection, the cosmos is devoid of its most fundamental meaning without the person and destiny of Jesus Christ. What has happened in him is a new creation—a deeper, fuller level of being. Creation and redemption are not simply identical, but neither are they totally unrelated. Creation is the placing of the beginning of that which finds its full consummation in the redemptive mystery of Christ. Redemption is the saving completion of the world of God's creation, which is intimately related to the history of grace and the history of Christ and the church. Christ is the Lord who, from eternity, is involved in God's creative intention, who has redeemed the world in the fullness of time, and who, as the glorified Lord, leads it on to communion with God.

Theological Tradition

Such a reading of the biblical texts must be followed by a similar approach to the texts of the theological tradition. As a historical reading of the Bible helps to shed considerable light on the nature of the biblical faith and its relation to mythical expressions, so the historical readings of the later tradition will shed light on the confrontation of Christian faith with a variety of philosophical visions of the world. It must be somehow explained that traditional theology does not simply repeat the worldview implicit in Genesis, though some elements of it do, in fact, remain. Christians throughout the centuries have had to confront the claims of a variety of pantheisms, dualisms, and monisms. Out of such confrontations emerged the characteristic Christian theology of creation.

In arguing against the Gnostic dualism of his day, Irenæus of Lyons created an impressive form of Christocentric creation theology that echoed many Pauline themes. Christ is seen as the fullness of time, the high point and decisive grace-filled moment of history. It is in him that the human race finds its head. All of creation and its history are directed to him from the beginning. Christ "recapitulates" humanity and the whole of creation together with its history. The Incarnation is the beginning and the source of the unification of reality that takes place in the deification of humanity through grace and is consummated in the general resurrection. In his own time and place, Irenæus carried on the biblical tradition of theological reflection on history.

Forms of this Christocentric, historically oriented theology of creation were to become characteristic of Eastern patristic theology.[10]

---

10   J. Meyendorff, *Christ in Eastern Christian Thought* (Washington, 1969).

This style of theology would find its outstanding Western formulation much later in the thirteenth century work of Saint Bonaventure.[11] Perhaps no one in the history of Western thought has glimpsed the profound unity between the created world and Christ as consistently as did this great Franciscan for whom the whole of the world and its history constitutes a magnificent Christophany. Unfortunately, much of the grandeur of this deeply theological vision would be eclipsed by the more metaphysical style introduced in the West through the influence of Aristotle.

Another aspect of the theological tradition rests in that through the confrontation with forms of dualism and monism, theology entered into dialogue with various philosophical worldviews, elements of which would become building blocks of various styles of theology. Thus, much of Eastern patristic theology and Western theology from Augustine onward would employ fundamental notions of neo-Platonism to give a relatively coherent understanding of the world as a created reality. In a similar way, the Middle Ages wrestled with the problems raised by the philosophy of Aristotle, and gradually incorporated elements of Aristotelian metaphysics within Christian theology as basic structural elements. One of the implications of this is that although in the Hebrew Scriptures creation theology expressed itself in terms of the prescientific worldview of the ancient world, now it expressed itself partly in those terms, but partly and even more decisively in terms of either Platonism or Aristotelianism. As worldviews change, the particular shape of the theology of creation changes as well. A comparison between Aquinas, Irenæus, and the Hebrew Scriptures would demonstrate this with dramatic clarity.

The reading of the theological tradition in light of the ongoing confrontation of faith with various philosophical viewpoints led to the possibility of singling out the central concerns of tradition and distinguishing them from the details of the physical cosmology that is clearly operative in the structure of theology. While some of the more general features of this cosmology such as the geocentric vision of the cosmos are familiar to us, many of its details have faded into oblivion in the popular mind, even though they have left their impression on

---

11 This is clearly expressed in two important works of Bonaventure: the *Itinerarium* and the *Hexæmeron* in *Works of Bonaventure*, tr. J. De Vinck (Paterson, NJ, 1960–69) vols. I & V.

Christian religious language in many ways. In terms of this cosmology, theologians were accustomed to distinguishing the ten heavenly spheres that surrounded the earth and the four spheres of elemental nature. Beginning at the lowest level were the basic elements of earth, water, air, and fire associated with the qualities of dryness, wetness, cold, and heat. Next were the seven planetary spheres, which included five of the planets familiar to us together with the sun and the moon. Above this was the firmament of the stars, and then the crystalline heavens. At the summit was the empyrean sphere of fire or pure light. All this was seen to be organized in supreme order and beauty, being in its own way an expression of the Creator.

Against the background of this cosmology and in dialogue with the various philosophical visions concerning the nature of the world and of the place of human beings in the world, Christian theology developed what might be called an alternate theological-metaphysical vision of the nature of the world, which, to a great extent, is synthesized in the term *creation from nothing.*

In its most basic sense, this term is a theological attempt to express the conviction that God is the sole source of all existence.[12] God as Creator is the mystery of absolute origin; God is the ground of existence as such. Finite existence as we find it in the individual and multiple beings of the world derives not from some primal cataclysm, nor from some primeval conflict between opposed principles of good and evil, nor from some prehistorical rupture of primordial unity, but from the loving will of a Creator God. To exist as a finite being and as an individual being in a world of multiplicity is not an evil but a gift and a responsibility given by a loving, creative God. In this theological-metaphysical conviction is grounded the Christian confidence in the goodness and the redeemability of life.

The *nothing* of which this formula speaks is not some preexistent formless matter, nor the divine substance itself, but simply and absolutely nonexistence. To say that God creates from nothing implies that there is no direct analogy from any human art that can be used to express the nature of God's creative act, for no finite act confers existence as such, which is precisely what is said of God's creative act. Even the category of *cause,* which is commonly used in

---

12 Gilkey, *Maker of Heaven and Earth: The Christian Doctrine of Creation in the Light of Modern Knowledge* (Garden City, 1959, 1965 pbk.), p. 49.

this context, must be carefully qualified. In Scholastic terms, God is a cause in a unique sense of the word. God is not a cause among causes, nor an extension of inner worldly causes; God is not the first link in the chain of causes that are studied by the scientists. God is the cause of being as such (primary causality), whereas all the causes that we experience in space and time (secondary causes) are the causes of the concrete forms of being in individual existence. In terms of the category of causality, the Creator-God is not a cause within the world, nor a cause who stands at the first moment of the history of the world, but the abiding ground of inner worldly being and causality at all times. Whether we choose to use the category of causality or any other category, no model can adequately express the creative act of God as the conferral of existence after simple nonexistence.

While we use a variety of models such as causality, making, or emanation to say something about how the world comes to be, these are of limited usefulness and fade into the background in the face of what appears to be a far more significant question; namely, *why* does God create? This sort of question is more important because it is at this level that the real question of meaning arises. While one may come to no clear understanding of the purpose of created existence from the contemplation of the world alone, theology sees an answer to this question in the Scriptures, and most particularly in the mystery of Christ. If it is true to say that the destiny of created existence is realized in an anticipatory way in the destiny of the glorified Christ, then theology can conclude that the purpose or goal of created existence is the realization of a loving, transforming union of the creature with the Creator such as has been realized in the Incarnation and glorification of Christ.

To perceive the world in these terms is to perceive something about the nature of God as well. God creates for this purpose because the divine being is, in itself, a mystery of self-communicative love. Thus Irenæus could write: "God creates so as to have someone on whom to confer the gift of goodness."[13] Augustine echoes this in his own way: "Because God is good, we exist."[14] God creates not to gain something for the divine being itself, but for the gain of creatures.

---

13 *Adversus haereses*, IV, 14.
14 *De doctrina Christian*, I, 32, 35.

Viewed in this way, creation can be seen as a personal process flowing from a personal, loving God that results in personal creatures who are ordered to personal, loving union with the creative ground of their being. This personalistic understanding of created reality stands in striking contrast with most forms of monism and dualism for which personal, finite being is derived in some way from an impersonal Absolute. It is in this theological understanding of creation that the Christian hope in the fulfillment of individual and multiple existence is grounded. Fulfillment is seen to consist in a transforming union of love in which the individual and multiple are not absorbed into formless identity with the Absolute but are most fully defined in their individual existence as other than the Absolute.

The understanding of creation as purposive is further qualified by the understanding of God as one who is both intelligence and will. Finite existence, from this perspective, may be seen as a "being known and being loved into existence" by the creative ground of all. Hence, meaning and purpose are not peripheral qualities of finite existence, but are deeply rooted in the fact of existence as such. While the theology of creation recognizes the world as good in its basic reality, it sees this as a participatory goodness. Therefore, neither the world as a whole nor any individual being within the world can be invested with absolute meaning.

As a theological concept, the notion of *creation from nothing* is an attempt to express the real ground of the Christian confidence in life. As an alternate metaphysical position, it involves the denial of ultimate irrationality, which is replaced with faith in meaning and purpose. In as far as it sees value in the essential structure of the concrete existent, it opens to us the possibility that every dimension of our finite being is potentially meaningful and will be involved in the realization of human fulfillment. It offers a vision for liberating humanity from any impersonal, deterministic interpretation of the world and presents an understanding in which the free, creative work of humanity in history can be seen as ultimately meaningful.[15] As a vision of the world and of human life, it stands in striking contrast to all forms of nihilism and fatalism.

---

15 Gilkey, *Maker of Heaven and Earth*, pp. 178–200.

This theological vision can be distinguished from the physical image of the world described earlier as well as from the metaphysical visions of either Plato or Aristotle. While the development of this theological notion employed elements from both Plato and Aristotle, in both cases Christian theology had to make significant changes in the philosophical visions bequeathed to it from the world of antiquity.

The theological notion of creation may be seen as the fruit of the development of religious consciousness moving from its original religious experience and attempting to conceptualize the conditions that must occur if that religious experience is to be taken as a genuine disclosure of saving reality. If the religious experience is truly the opening of a saving, healing relation to the world and to God, then it must mean something about the nature of the world and of God. The theological concept of *creation from nothing* is an attempt to conceptualize those implications. It commits theology definitively to neither the physical cosmology nor to the metaphysical systems of antiquity.

From this sort of historical awareness arises another shift in theological concern. Namely, if physical cosmology undergoes change, will this have any implications for theology? If theology will inevitably express the concerns of faith in terms of some scientific and philosophical worldview, and if there is no particular scientific or philosophical worldview that is binding as the content of revelation, what form will a creation theology take if it should assume the task of speaking in terms of the twenty-first-century experience of the world?

For many theologians this has come to mean asking about the possibility of constructing theology in reference to the modern experience of the history of the cosmos as perceived in the modern sciences. For many it seems that the historical character of the modern experience of a world-in-process has a greater affinity with the vision of the Bible than does the physical and metaphysical view of Aristotle, which has been the major dialogue partner of Christian theology for seven hundred years. What possibilities are there of retrieving the "forgotten truth" of a Christocentric history of creation and salvation and relating it to the historically experienced world mediated to us not only by scientists and philosophers but by television, movies, and popular news magazines on all sides? An honest and intelligent reading of the literary sources of our theological tradition will at least allow us to ask such a question with full seriousness and will encourage us in our attempt to deal with it.

– 3 –

A New Shape
for the General Doctrine
of Creation

Shifts in focus concerning both Scripture and the later tradition underscore the traditional basis for affirming (1) the relation between creation and salvation, and (2) the relation between Christ and creation. Catholic thought has been affected in two principal ways. Creation is no longer thought of as an event that happened long ago to be followed by God's preservation of the world. Indeed, the Scholastic notions of creation in the primary and in the secondary sense are brought much closer together. Creation is seen as the initiation of God's salvific involvement with the world and its history. Related to this, the cosmic significance of the mystery of Christ is elaborated in relation to the doctrine of creation. Dialogue between these elements of the theological tradition and some version of the modern experience of the world is leading to an overall restructuring of the ideas generally treated as the general doctrine of creation. This is taking shape in line with the temporal dimensions of the modern experience of the world. Within this restructured framework, particular issues are treated in a fresh way, specifically the origin of the human race and the origin of sin and evil. This chapter treats first the general framework of the restructuring and then the particular questions regarding biological evolution and sin.

Fragmentary Attempts

As we might expect, the confrontation between faith and the modern world experience has taken place in some rather hesitant steps leading to fragmentary presentations. To recognize this is not to belittle the efforts of modern theology. It is simply to find in our own day the same sort of development that took place in the twelfth and thirteenth centuries in the major confrontation between faith and worldview represented in the physics, metaphysics, and ethics of Aristotle. Only after many hesitant and fragmentary forays in the direction of that unfamiliar terrain was the mighty synthesis of Aquinas possible.

Most Protestant theologians who have made contributions in this area have done so under the express influence of the process philosophy of Whitehead and Hartshorne. Thus, J. B. Cobb has developed natural theology in terms of the Whiteheadian philosophy.[1] Cobb deals with the question of conceiving of God and the divine action in the world in terms of a philosophy which is explicitly related to twentieth-century physics. Similarly, R. Overman has sketched the broad outlines of a new framework for the theological task within which he discusses the particular question of evolutionary theory.[2] Both Cobb and Overman share the conviction common to process theologians that such a philosophical framework provides a model for conceiving of the relation between the world and God in terms that are more compatible with the biblical witness than is the Aristotelian model with which Christian theology has long been familiar. Both seek to conceive the creative action of God in terms of an ongoing relation to the world of great intimacy, feeling that such a view not only relates to the modern experience of the world-in-process but also to the scriptural confession of a God involved in the history of creation.

Roman Catholic theologians have been less eager to adopt Whitehead as their philosophical dialogue partner. To varying degrees, they have come under the influence of the controversial

---

1 *A Christian Natural Theology, Based on the Thought of Alfred N. Whitehead.* (Philadelphia, 1965).

2 *Evolution and the Christian Doctrine of Creation: A Whiteheadian Interpretation.* (Philadelphia, 1968).

Jesuit, Teilhard de Chardin. This is especially clear in the case of P. Schoonenberg and A. Hulsbosch.[3]

Both take as the dominant characteristic of the modern world experience the fact of flux, change, and novelty. This stands in sharp contrast with the classical theological formulation of the world in terms of stability and substantial reality. We are reminded of the contrast between Parmenides and Heraclitus. The one emphasizes stability and situates change within the framework of potency and act. The other emphasizes change and situates whatever stability there may be within the dynamics of becoming. Our familiar theology is cast in terms of the former. The challenge of theology today is raised by the dominance of the latter in our culture.

Viewed in this way, the principal question is not whether theology can appropriate some form of biological evolution, but the larger question of whether it can appropriate a modern Heraclitean world experience. If this can be carried out at all, it will mean a fundamental shift from the notion that God creates a finished world at the beginning of time to the notion that the creativity of God is revealed in a world that is in the process of becoming what it is not yet.

Working from quite a different orientation, Rahner provides a theology of history that is neither directly Teilhardian nor Whiteheadian, but far more akin to the philosophy of Hegel and German idealism. Its focus is not so much on the history of the physical world but more on the history of the human spirit within the world.[4] Thus, while Rahner does at times deal with questions that have a specifically scientific reference (e.g., the problem of monogenism in theology), the physical sciences play a rather minimal role in his thought as a whole. Yet he does deal with a vision of the world somehow taken up in a historical process in the dialectics of matter and spirit and attempts to retrieve something of the Scotistic theology of the absolute predestination of Christ in reference to such a historical experience of the world.[5] It is in the history of the human spirit,

---

3 P. Schoonenberg, *God's World in the Making*. Duquesne Studies: Theological Studies, 2 (Pittsburgh, 1964); A. Hulsbosch, *God's Creation: Creation, Sin and Redemption in an Evolving World*. tr. M. Versfeld (London, 1965 pbk).

4 *Hominisation*, pp. 46–61 on spirit and matter; pp. 62–93 on the concept of becoming.

5 *Theological Investigations* V, "Christology Within an Evolutionary View of the World" (London, 1968) pp. 157–192.

individually and collectively, that the history of the world becomes a conscious and self-directing history; it is in the person of Jesus Christ that the fundamental meaning of that history is found. In such a context, creation is the placing of the beginnings of that which finds its ultimate meaning in Christ. Rahner can speak of this history without committing himself to any specific form of evolutionary theory, but simply to the incompleteness of the world's history in the human race.

Gathering the Fragments

All these statements have been provocative but essentially fragmentary and incomplete. Perhaps the most sustained attempt to map out the contours of a new theological model is the little-known study of R. Pendergast entitled *Cosmos*.[6] Recognizing his indebtedness to Teilhard, Rahner, and Whitehead, Pendergast builds on the stimulation they have provided. He comes at this task with an unusual background, holding degrees in the fields of philosophy, theology, and science, and he has woven themes from all these disciplines into a thought-provoking cosmic vision that is distinctly modern. Within a general view of the world reflecting the insights of atomic science and astrophysics, Pendergast describes the cosmic locale of the human phenomenon and discusses the significance of human consciousness and symbolic activity in such a world. Here he reveals the influence of Rahner. Within such a general view of the world, he treats the meaning of creation and predestination, sin and evil, hope and eschatology. Throughout, he expresses the implications of the basic conviction that dynamic process is a fundamental feature of cosmic reality that theology ignores only at a great price.

The theological conceptualization of creation as elaborated by Pendergast reveals the influence of Whitehead. God creates a field of possibilities with a goal or purpose. Which of these possibilities become actualities is worked out in the historical interaction of secondary causes. When humanity comes into the picture, the actualization of possibilities involves the exercise of human freedom. The realization of God's ideal purpose, therefore, is internally related to

---

6 *Cosmos* (NY, 1973).

the quality of created choices. The outcome of history involves both the action of God, who provides possibilities to creation, and the creaturely response to the possibilities that God opens to creation. The quality of the future, therefore, depends on how closely human choices coincide with God's ideal aim. While in terms of existence, God is independent of the world, it is precisely this transcendence with respect to existence that makes it possible for God to choose freely to be dependent on the world in another sense, that is, in working out the divine purpose for the world.

The Whiteheadian overtones of this view become even clearer in the reformulation of such notions as divine perfection and divine knowledge and power. While our familiar theology thinks of God's perfection as analogous to a rock that resists all change, Pendergast defines it in terms that reflect the Whiteheadian doctrine of relation, choosing the analogy of human perfection that is characterized by openness to interaction and relationship. God's perfection could be described in the following way. Since God is constant in terms of the divine being, the divine manner of relating to the world is constant, always holding open a range of possibilities including the best, for the purpose of evoking the qualitative development of life. But God is affected by creaturely decisions. Therefore, God is vulnerable in working out the ideal, divine aim. Instead of speaking about the omniscience of God, Pendergast, following the lead of Whitehead, prefers to call God's knowledge "adequate" or "appropriate to reality." This means that God knows the real as real, but the possible as possible. Therefore, when a possibility has been realized as an actuality, God knows it as real. With respect to God's power, instead of thinking of God as one who can do anything that does not involve an intrinsic contradiction, Pendergast prefers to see God as one who has "limited himself" by risking the sort of creation whose success depends on free, human choices.

The influence of Teilhard may be seen in the way the cosmos is related to Christ. The cosmos is seen principally as a process, but the meaning of any process is determined by its end. The material world finds a new level of being and meaning in the world of life. The world of life finds greater being and depth in conscious, personal life. Conscious, personal life finds its depth not in isolated human monads but in the emergence of a human community of love. Teilhard's Christ stands at the pinnacle of this universe as the one who brings to the world the phylum of love that provides the true direction for the convergence of the human community around its center. Thus, Pendergast's vision of the created world culminates, much as does that of the Scriptures, with an eschatological vision of a world transformed through the power of love—a Christified world.

Evaluation

All the above are attempts to create, in whole or in part, a new framework for the theology of creation. All these authors reflect the common conviction that a changed experience of the world requires a corresponding change in theology. All are expressions of the hope for a new synthesis of faith and concrete worldview. The fundamental problem is that it is not yet clear what will provide an adequate basis for such a synthesis. The anthropocentric and evolutionary concerns of Teilhard need critical refinement, but they are certainly suggestive of rich possibilities for theology and for Christian life and spirituality. For some theologians, the philosophy of Whitehead seems to provide an apt tool for dealing with the questions and suggestions of evolutionary thought patterns. For others, such as Rahner, a critical recovery of some form of German idealism would seem to serve the purpose. But most important is that there are those in the community of faith who are willing to take up the task at all.

Many details of such attempts are unclear and problematic. But for our purposes here, it is sufficient to make some broader evaluations. The creation of such a framework would have some obvious positive effects. Since it speaks in language that is understandable in terms of contemporary experience, it does not require that believers, who are modern in their daily experience, must become medieval or even premedieval in the world of faith. Even though such a theology speaks in terms of the concrete forms of the world process, it retains its nature as theology in so far as it reflects on the fact that anything exists in the first place to be in process (creation from nothing). This new framework for the theology of creation recognizes the radically contingent nature of the world and all in it, and hence it perceives the basic nature of creation as a gift. The negative statement that the world is created from nothing implies the positive statement that the world is totally from God in terms of its being. As a result, the world is totally the real symbol of the loving freedom of God.

Without identifying grace with evolution, this framework engages the historical sensitivity of a modern worldview with the concerns of salvation history. It conceives the deep unity between the destiny of the world and the destiny of the human race.[7] In this regard, such a theology would provide helpful impulses for an important social-critical function. We are now aware of the dangers of a philosophy of unlimited development and exploitation of nature. The environmental problems and ecological questions of our times are sufficient witness to the questionable character of such a philosophy. The awareness of the created character of the world can add a dimension of sensitivity that is crucial to our human future in the world. For creation-faith understands the world is given as a gift. It is not a mere brute fact to be exploited at the whim of the technologist. As a gift, it is to be accepted with respect and responsibility as an expression of the loving will of God. A theology of creation speaking of this religious insight in terms of the modern world experience can fulfill an important function in the human endeavor to find new norms and criteria for our relation to the world.

One may object that such attempts are ill advised because they take as their dialogue partner a view of the world that is not sufficiently verified by science, or that is not universally accepted by science. It is true that there is no universally accepted scientific worldview. But this ought not to obscure that certain qualities of our experience appear in any modern view of the world. Among these is the understanding of the structure of the world as related systems from the world of the atom to the galaxies, as well as the sense of being in a history of which the human race is a part. About such facts theology must be willing to speak. Our failure to do so runs the risk of making Christianity incapable of communicating anything of importance to believers and nonbelievers whose psyche is shaped, for better or for worse, by these factors.

Finally, it may be argued that such a relation between faith and science results in a fragile sort of theology, for it is tied to a scientific view that itself is subject to change. Must theology change at the whim

---

7 Rm. 5:12ff.; 8:19ff.

of science? We are not suggesting that science provides the basis for theology. Theology emerges from religious experience and revelation, not from scientific proof. But if religious experience is to enter into dialogue with the world at large, it must make use of concepts drawn from the culture around it. Thus, important as theology is, it is yet a fragile, human undertaking. This has always been the case as often as Christians have attempted to develop a theology of creation in terms of the concrete world of their experience. The reason this does not seem to be evident is that we too easily forget where earlier theological world images came from. Likewise, we have forgotten many of the details of the world as conceived by earlier theologies (e.g., the medieval concept of the planetary spheres). As a result, we are often unaware of the extent to which such secular views have shaped our familiar religious language. We can also point out that the major contours of such a world image do not change overnight. Indeed, the basic thrust of the modern experience has been in the making for centuries, at least from the time of the Renaissance. While details within the larger framework will no doubt change quickly, it is with the larger framework itself that we are concerned.

-4-

Creation and the Origin of the Human Race

It is within the general change of worldview from the classical view to that of the modern world that the particular question of the evolutionary origin of the human race is situated. This is an issue that has undergone rather striking development since the 1950s, reaching a high point around 1960. Though other particular theological issues are related to this, we will limit our remarks for now to the question of evolution as seen in theological terms. This problem breaks down into two specific questions: that of the general acceptability of the biological evolution of the human race, and more specifically that of the monogenetic or polygenetic understanding of the theory of evolution.

General Acceptability of Evolution

One may recall not only the monkey trial in which William Jennings Bryan locked horns with Clarence Darrow but also the writings of many reputable representatives of the Roman Catholic tradition who argued that anything like the evolution of species, to say nothing of the evolution of the human species, was impossible and clearly in conflict with the Bible.[1] In 1958, Karl Rahner remarked that

---

1   Many Roman Catholic theologians of the nineteenth century considered moderate evolution as dangerous and even as heretical. In 1895, M. D. Leroy had to retract his view approving a moderate evolution as did P. Zahn in 1899. The change in the theological climate may be seen in that even such careful authors

theological opinion will "change very rapidly in favor of freedom to maintain a theory of evolution."[2] At the present, most mainstream theologians in the major Christian traditions of the West find some form of evolutionary theory to be acceptable. The situation alluded to by Rahner has become a reality more quickly than most would have expected.

The actual course that evolution has taken is first and foremost a question of the sciences such as biology, anthropology, paleontology, etc. The principal task of theology in terms of the general theory of evolution is to clarify why there is no conflict between the theological concept of "creation from nothing" and the emergence of the concrete forms of created beings through some sort of evolutionary process. In terms of the three levels of questions described in chapter 1, the actual description of the evolutionary process pertains to the level of cause-and-effect relations in the framework of space and time. This is legitimately the concern of the sciences. On the other hand, the notion of "creation from nothing" pertains to the question, arising from the world of religion and shaped in metaphysical terms, as to how it happens that there is anything to evolve at all. In this sense, it can be said that the concept of creation and evolution are not in conflict or competition with each other. They speak to two quite distinct levels of questioning. The notion of creation is by far the more fundamental of the two. It expresses the most basic condition for the possibility of evolution, while evolution itself describes the actual temporal-spatial effect of God's creative action. In brief, God creates through evolution.

This can be expressed in another way from Scholastic theology. The Scholastics spoke of primary and secondary causality. Secondary causality is the Scholastic term for the entire realm that we understand to be the concern of the sciences. It refers to all the cause-and-effect relations that constitute the world in its concrete form. Primary causality, on the other hand, is the unique causality of God as the very ground of being. Primary causality points to the mystery of being as

---

as M. Schmaus and J. Hardon recognize the possible acceptability of some form of moderate evolution. Cfr. M. Schmaus, *Dogma 2: God and Creation*, tr. Læuchli, McKenna, Burke. (NY, 1969) pp. 110–144, J. Hardon, *The Catholic Catechism* (Garden City, 1975) p. 93.

2 *Hominisation*, p. 30.

such, whereas secondary causality points to the emergence of being in precisely this concrete form.

To understand the world as a created world is to understand it in terms of both levels of causality. God is not a cause among the secondary causes, but the ground for the fact that there is causality in the world at all. On the other hand, the actual, concrete form that beings possess must take into account the interaction of cause and effect in all the concrete dimensions of existence. This is the meaning of the paradoxical Scholastic conviction that effects within the world are "totally of God" and simultaneously "totally of the creature." While Scholastic thought tended to explain the emergence of something new in terms of the metaphysics of potency and act, contemporary theology tends to explain it in terms of evolutionary theory. Contrary to the fears of many Christians, the concept of evolution as such does not eliminate God since it does not pretend to speak of primary causality but only of secondary causality.

The questions and fears aroused for generations of Christians by evolutionary thought have had a positive effect. They have helped correct a tendency to deism in the popular understanding of creation and have facilitated the recovery of the traditional theological conviction of God's proximity to the world. By deism, we mean the view holding that God created the world in the beginning but has had little if anything to do with the world after the act of creation. It is as though God wound up the immense cosmic clock, which subsequently winds itself out with no further concern on the part of God. Clearly a theology that takes evolutionary patterns seriously will be inclined to conceive the relation of God to the world in far more intimate terms. In fact, the Scholastic notions of creation and conservation are brought into far greater proximity by Christian evolutionists. As long as there is history, God is active as Creator. Under the stimulus of evolutionary thought, modern theology has escaped from the tendency to deism and has recovered a greater sense of the immanence of the God who is transcendent.

We have said that some form of evolution has gained acceptability by mainstream theologians. This distinguishes the notion of evolution from particular forms of scientific theory that in fact do exclude God from their picture of reality. Forms of radical materialistic, atheistic evolution are in conflict with theology. This is not because of the notion of evolution as such, but because of the non-scientific bias with which the concept is filled out and interpreted.

Monogenism and Polygenism

Whether the human race stems from one couple or from many is clearly a question that can be dealt with directly only by the sciences. This being the case, it may seem surprising at first that it should be discussed by theologians. The reason for this theological concern is not that theologians have some particular data to add to that of the sciences concerning the concrete beginnings of the human race. Rather, the biological question seems to have implications for questions of a directly theological nature. The question at issue here is the theological problem of the universality of sin.

The classical theological formulation of the doctrine of original sin long supposed that the only way one could seriously affirm the universality of sin was to affirm the biological connection of all human beings with the first human couple. This long-standing interpretation of the doctrine also included an interpretation of two scriptural texts that seemed to be particularly pertinent to the question. Interpreting the text of Genesis, chapters 2–3, in a flatly historical sense, theologians for many generations saw this text as a description of the first human couple from whom all human beings descended biologically. They had no reason to see the matter in any other way. The Hebrew Scriptures seemed to be confirmed by Romans 5:12–19, which was interpreted to mean that Adam was the first father of all human beings. This seemed to be the obvious and unquestionable meaning of the passage that reads: "Therefore, just as through one person sin entered the world, and through sin, death, and thus death came to all, inasmuch as all sinned" (Rm. 5:12). Not only do these texts clearly seem to teach the monogenetic origins of the human race, but the text of Romans seems to associate this vision of origins directly with original sin. Or so it was long supposed.

It is because of this connection between a biological theory and a specifically theological concern that theologians have felt the need to speak concerning the scientific positions suggested in recent years. Once the question of the biological evolution of the human race is entertained as a serious possibility, the question of polygenism must be faced because, from a scientific point of view, if evolution is accepted, the idea of monogenetic evolution is awkward at best. Yet if the possibility of polygenism is entertained, what are we to say of the Church's doctrine concerning original sin? In 1950, Pope Pius XII, in his encyclical *Humani generis*, spoke on the issue in carefully nuanced terms. With careful restrictions, the pope writes: "The teaching of the church leaves the doctrine of evolution an open question."[3] The restrictions that the pope described were such as to limit the discussion to the evolution of the human body from other living matter, for, according to this encyclical, it is necessary to hold that God creates the soul immediately, even though one might entertain the evolutionary origin of the body. This area, writes the pope, is a legitimate concern of both scientific and theological research that should seriously weigh the evidence for and against the theory. It is not, in the eyes of the pope, a closed issue, either from the viewpoint of science or from that of theology.

The same sort of freedom of debate is not accorded to the theory of polygenism, which is explicitly mentioned in the encyclical. It is at this point that the pope draws the explicit connection between the doctrine of original sin and monogenism. It seems, according to this view, that only the actual biological connection between the first couple and subsequent generations can adequately ground the doctrine of the universal sinfulness of the human race. Thus, the pope does not explicitly exclude the possibility of studying the question. But he clearly expresses the condition that must be met by any attempt to reconcile polygenism with the doctrine of the church. "For it is not clear how such views can be reconciled with the doctrine of original sin."[4]

While in some quarters, this text was seen to put an end to the possibilities of recognizing any form of polygenism, a careful reading of it justifies the conclusion that it is a strong warning to which a particular condition is attached. But what if it should become clear that there are possibilities of reconciling the biological theory of polygenism with the teaching of the Church? It is necessary first for

---

3   J. Neuner and H. Roos, *The Teaching of the Catholic Church* (Staten Island, 1967) pp. 124–126.

4   Ibid., p. 126.

theology to deal with the texts of Genesis and Romans, which seem to speak clearly of monogenetic origins. After some comments on the exegetical studies of these texts, we will give some indication of how modern theologians tend to discuss the relation of sin to the unity of the human race.

Our remarks on the biblical texts will be limited to the most general sort. A more detailed statement will be given with the discussion of original sin. We have pointed out above that the flat, historical interpretation of Genesis has disappeared from virtually all theological presentations outside strictly fundamentalist circles. For Rahner, the Genesis account is to be seen as historical etiology. This means that although the account is largely fictional in character and contains many symbolic and mythical elements, it represents an attempt to express the historical cause of the human experience of the ongoing conflict between good and evil. The experience of fundamental goodness is traced to the theological claim that the world is the gift of God's creative love. The experience of evil, on the other hand, is traced to the historical way human beings have responded to God through the exercise of their freedom. While the Genesis account is not to be taken in a flat, historical sense, it does, in Rahner's view, speak of the historical cause of the presence of sin and evil in the world. Rahner sees this to involve a first sin that initiated the sinfulness of the human race.[5] Hulsbosch, on the other hand, sees the account as pure etiology in which no particular historical facts are involved.[6] In this view, the origin of human sinfulness lies not in any particular sin, but in the sum total of sins in human history. While Rahner's view reflects a clear concern for the traditional concept of an individual first sin, Hulsbosch sees this to be of little or no concern. In fact, for Hulsbosch, it is not at all necessary to have any concrete image of how the human race came into being and what specific historical events may have happened in the beginning of human history.

Most mainstream theologians would tend to align themselves with Rahner's position or with something similar to it. The present assessment of the situation could be summarized in the conviction that there is nothing in the book of Genesis that binds theology unequivocally

---

5 "Evolution and Original Sin," in *Concilium* 26 (Glen Rock, NJ, 1967) pp. 61–73.

6 *God's Creation: Creation, Sin and Redemption in an Evolving World*, pp. 15–57; 118–145.

and definitively to the view that the human race springs from one and only one original couple. Thus, Z. Alszeghy and M. Flick write: "Exegetes incline to say that all that is taught in Genesis 3 is that the spread of evil (especially moral evil) in humankind stems from a willful resistance to God's will. All the rest (the state of original justice, the unicity of the sinful couple, the physical descent of all humans from that couple) does not belong to the message of Genesis.[7]

Concerning the teaching of Romans, S. Lyonnet concludes that Adam is mentioned with reference to the meaning of Christ, to make that meaning better understood, to justify it, and to explain it to a certain extent. Adam's culpability, the universality of sin, and the solidarity of all humans are to Paul facts commonly known and proven from Scripture. They are not ends, but rather presuppositions and means.[8] H. Haag summarizes the exegetical understanding of Romans by affirming that the literal understanding of the Fall is no more the object of Paul's teaching than the literal understanding of Jonah is the object of Christ's teaching.[9] In reference to the relation of Adam to Christ, P. Lengsfeld writes: "In the typology Adam-Christ, nothing, really nothing, can be affirmed as to the historical individuality of the figure of Adam."[10]

In general, we may conclude that at the present state of exegetical and theological understanding, no scriptural text taken by itself demands the acceptance of biological monogenism. What is principally at stake in the doctrine of original sin is that the sinful condition of humanity is a historical state rather than an essential condition. It is, further, a universal condition affecting all, and in some way humankind is accountable for it. Whereas this expresses the experience of sin in human history as perceived by the authors of the Hebrew Scriptures, the Christian Scriptures associate this directly with the experience of universal salvation in Christ. Thus in the Pauline materials cited, the universality of sin is a function of the prior conviction of the universality of redemption in Christ.

---

7 "Il peccato originale in prospettiva evoluzionistica," in *Gregorianum* 47 (1966) pp. 201–225.

8 "Das Problem der Erbsünde im Neuen Testament," in *Stimmen der Zeit* 7 (1967) p. 35.

9 *Biblische Schöpfungslehre and kirchliche Erbsündenlehre* (Stuttgart, 1966) p. 61.

10 *Adam und Christus: Die Adam-Christus Typologie im Neuen Testament und ihre Verwendung bei M. J. Scheeben und Karl Barth* (Essen, 1965) p. 115.

Having cleared the ground, to some degree, by these reflections on the understanding of the scriptural texts, we can now proceed directly to the question of the relation between biological polygenism and the doctrine of original sin. It has become increasingly clear to theologians that it may be a mistake to depend too much on some supposed biological unity of the human race as the condition for the Church's teaching. Scripture seems to indicate a type of solidarity among human persons that is deeper and more meaningful than any presumed unity in the biological order. One thinks in this context of the words placed on the lips of John the Baptist that "God can raise up children to Abraham from these stones" (Mt. 3:9; Lk. 3:8). And even further, one thinks of the depth of the unity of the community of believers in the mystery of faith and grace in Jesus Christ.[11] Does this not indicate that a biological connection with Abraham or with Jesus is not the final basis of unity in the religious community of faith? Do such texts point at least to the possibility that our ultimate relations with God in terms of sin and grace may not necessarily be based on a common biological fact in our past, but even more on a common God-given destiny that lies ahead? Is it possible that what makes us all human is not that all are derived from the same earthly material through a biological chain of cause and effect, but that—regardless of how we came to be historically—we are all called to a common destiny in Christ through the gracious love of God? To the Christian evolutionist, therefore, the human race is indeed a unity. But the basis of its unity is located differently.

If it should become clear that the unity of the race may be adequately accounted for by this strategic shift of emphasis, then it should also be possible to render an account of the universality of sin in a new way. And paradoxically, it becomes less important what precise image of the concrete origins of humanity we may have.

Theological Anthropology

Two anthropological concerns have surfaced in recent theological reflections. The first is the question of human dignity, which seems

---

11 Paul knows of a solidarity based on a spiritual fact rather than on a physical, biological fact. Cf. Rm. 9:6–8; Gal. 3:7,9. Cf. J. de Fraine, *The Bible and the Origin of Man* (Staten Island, 1961) pp. 56–61.

to be threatened by the way evolution envisions our roots in the physical world. The second is the question of human dominion over the world of nature, which has become problematic in view of the environmental problems of our technological culture. In a basic sense, both have to do with the relation of humanity to the physical world that provides the context of human life and history.

Throughout the ages, biblical sources have provided inspiration for the theological understanding of the dignity of the human person and of our relation to the physical world. Among the many texts that bear on this topic, those of Genesis, chapters 1–3 stand out in the history of Christian theology. At this point, our earlier description of the historical development of creation-faith must be more carefully nuanced.

The present form of the Genesis texts may be the result of late redactional work, but it is seen to reflect two distinct traditions, each of which communicates a distinct theological vision. While the influence of covenant theology seems clear enough, these texts are seen to reflect also the influence of the teachers associated with the courts of David and Solomon. In particular, the experience of David, the good king, provides a paradigm for understanding the place of humanity in the world. And the experience of the less-fortunate Solomon provides insight into the sort of disaster that can emerge when humanity defines its relation to the world with little regard for the creatures that make it up.[12]

The anthropology of Genesis 1–3 is cast in kingly terms. The first chapter presents the creation of humanity as the crown of God's creative work that takes place on the sixth day. Of all the creatures that God has called into being, humanity alone is created in God's image and given the task of exercising a kingly role in the world. In the second chapter, God creates Adam and places him in the garden to till and tend it. It is as though humanity stands in the center, surrounded by all the creatures God has created to adorn the earth. The one who names the animals is also to work the earth at God's behest.

If we look at humanity from both perspectives, it appears that human dignity is grounded not so much in the fact that we are essentially unlike the animal world, but above all in the fact that somehow

---

12 W. Brueggemann, *In Man We Trust: The Neglected Side of Biblical Faith* (Richmond, 1972) pp. 29–63.

we are like God. It pertains to the essence of humanity to be ordered
to God. The concern of Genesis is not to reject any connection
between humanity and the nonhuman world, but to affirm the special
position and function of the human race within the world.

The history of theology reveals many attempts to interpret what
it means to say that we are created in the image of God. These interpretations are an attempt to pinpoint precisely in what aspect of
the human composite the image resides. It has been placed rather
commonly in the human soul or in some specific spiritual faculty of
the human person.

Recent exegetical studies emphasize that the biblical text does
not refer to some particular spiritual dimension, but designates the
whole of the human person in terms of a function or role that it is
to carry out within the created order. As C. Westermann argues, the
term *image* refers to the human person as a whole precisely in as
far as the person is a creature of God and somehow corresponds to
God. We are created in the image of God in order that something
can happen between God and ourselves, so that thus our lives may
receive meaning.[13]

Whereas the relation of humanity to God is the content of the
term *image*, our relation to the world is expressed in the injunction
to "have dominion" over it. This phrase also has been subjected to
a wide range of interpretations. In recent years, it has been seen
especially by Western Christians as a God-given mandate to engage
in the technological conquest of the physical world. While in one
sense, this had the advantage of relating the biblical tradition to the
increasingly secular trend of the modern world, in another sense it
had the dangerous consequence of divesting the biblical religious
tradition of any significant critical function in relation to the despoli-
ation of the environment that seems to be the inevitable consequence
of unlimited technological culture.

That this injunction has something to do with a certain form of
worldly consciousness can hardly be denied. Yet more recent studies
have uncovered a more accurate knowledge of the kind of metaphor
that is here being employed by the biblical authors. Recognizing the
influence of the experience of the Davidic and Solomonic kingship,

---

13   *Creation* (Philadelphia, 1974) p. 56.

Westermann argues that the meaning of the metaphor is to be drawn from the context of that experience.[14] Understood in such a context, the divine mandate is not a license to unlimited exploitation of nature. Rather, the metaphor emphasizes the qualities of a good king. Such a king is responsible for the good of the entire realm, and by carrying out his responsibility, the king mediates blessings and general well-being to the whole of the realm. Understood in this way, the metaphor expresses the close bond of humanity to the physical world together with human responsibility for the welfare of all things. In this view, the irresponsible exploitation of natural resources to the detriment of land, plant life, and animal life is not the exercise of dominion but precisely the opposite. Following a similar line of thought, Brueggemann interprets *dominion* to mean a caring relationship to the world. We are not free to make the world in the image of our greed and self-centeredness.[15] To be created in the image of God means that humanity is given a task or role to carry out. Through our relation to other persons and things in the world, we are to reflect something of God's creative love for the world. Our human relation to the world is to be the place where the mystery of God's creative love shines forth in visible creation. Such an anthropology clearly calls into question some of the basic values of technological culture.

While the first chapter of Genesis presents the dignity of humanity, the second and third chapters unite human dignity with human failure, and thus present in seminal form the basis of a far-reaching theological vision of polarities experienced in human existence.

The second chapter presents the origin of humanity by depicting God with the metaphor of a craftsman who forms the human being of the stuff of the earth and breathes into the lifeless form the breath of life. In highly symbolic form, the text presents the humble origins of humanity. The very name expresses our rootedness in the earth: *Adam*, that is, one who is of the earth. The earth is not foreign to us; we are drawn from the same matter present in the world around us. Yet we receive from God the gift of life.

It is particularly clear that Adam is not to live in isolation. Having roots in the earth, he stands in intimate relation to the material and

---

14   Ibid., p. 49.

15   *In Man We Trust*, pp. 74–81.

animal worlds. But above all, as seen in the creation of Eve, Adam is to live in human community. The anthropology of Genesis sees human life as one that must be worked out in a network of relations. This includes not only our relation to God, which is crucial, but our relation to the human world and the world of things whose destiny is tied to our own. The fundamental question of our relationship to God is so intimately intertwined with the meaning of human community in the biblical reflection that the two questions can hardly be separated. There is no one who exists only in relationship to God. A theological anthropology that approaches human existence as though this were possible is condemned to futility.

Thus, while chapter 1 of Genesis emphasizes strongly the dignity of humanity, chapter 2 clarifies that this should not lead to the idealization of the rugged individualist nor to the isolation of humanity from the world in which we live. We are of the world and have been entrusted with the care of the world. We are created by God to live a life in human community and in intimacy with the world around us. Such an anthropological vision is laden with implications for reflecting on the situation particularly in the Western world where the sense of the many levels of relations that make up human life has often yielded to an extreme form of individualism and disregard for the world of nature.

– 5 –

Original Sin

Sin and Religion in General

It is not mere chance that the opening chapters of the Bible describe the prelude to saving history in terms of the polarity of good and evil, for the experience of that polarity was a genuine factor in the ongoing experience of the Hebrew people. More generally, one of the functions of any religious system is to provide a context of meaning within which believers can come to terms with the major questions of human life, among which the problems of pain, suffering, and sin are major human concerns. Indeed, the basic experience that lies behind any religious attempt to deal with sin and evil is the underlying conviction that all is not well with the world.

Contemporary philosophers speak of the sense of estrangement or alienation. We are not what we ought to be. But from what are we alienated in the final analysis? From our own true identity? From other human persons? From the rest of the world? Are we alienated from all of these and perhaps from the very ground of our existence? The fundamental experience that underlies such language is a common human experience that is understood and interpreted in specific ways by diverse religious traditions. The question that concerns us here is that of the particular type of religious interpretation given to the common human experience of alienation, which was developed by the biblical tradition in the writings of the Hebrew and the Christian Scriptures and in subsequent Christian theological history. That which is spoken of as alienation or estrangement by philosophers is spoken of in the language of sin by Christian theology, which thereby interprets the cause of this experience in terms of its own particular understanding of God and of the relation between the human race and God.

In terms of the general systematic understanding of theology, the doctrine of sin is situated between the doctrine of creation and that of redemption because it is essentially an attempt to deal with the depth of our alienation from the personal ground of our being together with the possibility of overcoming that alienation. Theology speaks of sin at two distinct but related levels. First, individual actions and dispositions may be designated as sinful. At this level, there is a plurality of sins. Second, even more basic than that is an underlying, existential condition called sin. It is the state of being in which human persons find themselves to be isolated from the Holy. It is principally this sense of isolation from the Holy that concerns us here, for it is with this that the biblical tradition has wrestled in the attempt to interpret the sense of isolation in terms of its own experience of a personal, loving God.

The theological attempt to deal with this question has been communicated to us commonly in the form of the catechism presentation of the doctrine of original sin. The familiar form of this doctrine may be traced in its essential features to the work of Augustine. His work lived on in the decrees of several synods as well as in the work of Scholastic theology, and found a trimmed-down expression in the decrees of the Council of Trent. While leaving a number of questions open for theological discussion, Trent seems to have made no substantial changes in the Augustinian formulation of the doctrine. From the time of Trent until the advent of evolutionary thought patterns, Catholic theologians did little of significance in this sector of theology. However, with the emergence of historical consciousness and evolutionary thought patterns, many people had serious problems with a formulation that so clearly reflected an archaic worldview.

Influence of Augustine

A few brief remarks might serve to recall some of the characteristic features of the familiar presentation. While Augustine clearly recognized diverse levels of meaning in the texts of Genesis, one of those levels is—in his view—a clearly historical level whereby the description of Adam and Eve in the garden is seen as a description of two individual human beings, the first parents from whom all subsequent human beings are descended. They were created by God and established in a condition that far transcended any claims of their creaturely status. They were uniquely endowed with a supernatural gift of sanctifying grace together with other blessings called preternatural gifts. By virtue of these, they were immune from concupiscence, endowed with special gifts of knowledge, and free from the need to die. Although Augustine himself had envisioned a lengthy list of preternatural gifts, the common presentation has tended to limit them to the gifts of immortality, impassibility, integrity, miraculous knowledge, and freedom from error. While the Council of Trent maintained that Adam was "constituted in justice," it was far more circumspect with regard to the preternatural gifts than were many of the theologians who elaborated on Augustine's view. Trent speaks of some relation between sin and concupiscence, and sin and death, but it says little if anything else of the blissful state in the Garden of Eden.

Augustine's formulation was no doubt a major factor in the process whereby the story of Genesis was taken to be a historical description of an actual state of affairs somewhere on this earth. This blissful state of harmony and peace was disrupted by the sin of the first man, a sin which becomes all the more incomprehensible when one takes into account the remarkable endowments with which the first human was adorned by the Creator. Through sin, Adam lost not only sanctifying grace but all the preternatural gifts not only for himself but also for his posterity. The world was changed from a place of idyllic harmony to one of pain and agony. Immortality was lost, and a painful existence would be capped with a fearful death. While the individual sin of Adam must be distinguished from sin in his posterity, the situation to which we are heirs is characterized not only by the consequences of sin but by a situation of guilt as well.

The general contours of this picture of the beginnings of sin are familiar to most Christians and still tend to mediate the theological doctrine of original sin. Yet the fact that this vision is shaped clearly by the prescientific worldview of antiquity must raise many questions for those whose general worldview is deeply conditioned by the modern sciences. The most obvious sort of problem appears as soon as one attempts to associate this "historical description of the original state" of the human race with an evolutionary account of our biological origins. The familiar formulation envisions a higher state of perfection at the very beginning: Adam is, in effect, the perfect human being, certainly far more perfect than any of his posterity. On the other hand, an evolutionary view of human origins tends to envision rather simple beginnings followed by a growth toward better conditions. In an evolutionary view, the paradisial state as a historical condition is clearly a thorn in the side.

If the general idea of a state of perfection preceding the evolution from less perfect to more perfect forms of life is problematic, so also are the details of the description with which this notion of perfection was filled out in the familiar theological presentation. The classical view on the preternatural gifts is virtually incomprehensible as a description of a historical state.

If the emergence of evolutionary patterns has given rise to problems of this sort, they have also alerted us to other questions that have been long present but ignored. Does not the familiar presentation place an unwarranted emphasis on the first human being and the first sin almost in isolation from the real history of the race, which followed that first fateful deviation from God's will? Has the familiar account ever given a satisfactory explanation as to why the sin of one should have had such dreadful consequences for all?

If theologians today speak of reformulating the doctrine of original sin, it is not a question of rejecting an adequate theory and replacing it with another that may or may not be adequate. Rather, the familiar theory, which was laden with inadequacies from the start, has become almost incomprehensible for a Christian who views the origins of the human race in terms of some form of evolution. One cannot hold the possibility of some form of evolution without opening a Pandora's Box. Those who open that box must be willing to assume responsibility for dealing with the kinds of problems that emerge in many areas of theology. Up to the present, attempts of theology to reformulate the doctrine of original sin have been fragmentary, which is as it must be at this stage of development. Perhaps the time is not yet ripe for a synthesis. But from the various suggestions that have been made, we can begin to see certain common elements emerging that reveal something of a pattern for a future synthesis.

A New Look at the Sources

As we spoke of a fresh reading of the literary sources of the theological tradition with regard to the theology of creation, so here this is the first and most basic task which must be undertaken. As regards original sin, the familiar presentation is based largely on the texts of Genesis 2–3 and on Romans 5. These biblical sources together with the statements of the Council of Trent have been the principal textual sources with which modern theology has had to deal. Some reflections on each of these will help point to the direction in which theology is moving.

Genesis 2–3

Recent studies on the opening chapters of Genesis have shown the highly symbolic character of the texts and the many parallels that these accounts have with other religious texts of the Near East. It is generally accepted that the written form of the Bible did not begin with these accounts. Rather, the stories of the beginnings were shaped in their present form at a much later date. There is in the Hebrew Scriptures a highly developed theology of sin, the principal elements of which are brought together in an impressive way in the Genesis stories. For this reason, most exegetes and theologians are convinced that it is necessary to read these texts not in isolation, but in the larger context of the theology of sin found in the Hebrew Scriptures.[1]

Our intention is to single out a number of the more basic factors involved in the theology of sin and to point out their significance in the more recent interpretations of the Genesis account. One of the fundamental elements in the theology of sin is the feeling of a deep, pervasive presence of evil in a world that Israel believes to be the good creation of a good, loving God. The experience of evil in Israel's history stands in striking contrast with its fundamental belief in the saving presence of the God of the Covenant. So pervasive is evil and so deeply does it seem to be rooted in the human heart that it cannot be limited to particular acts. There seems to be good reason for speaking of an evil or sinful condition. The human heart

---

1 A. M. Dubarle, *The Biblical Doctrine of Original Sin*, tr. E. M. Stewart (NY, 1964); P. Schoonenberg, *Man and Sin: A Theological View*, tr. J. Donceel (Notre Dame, 1965).

is the seat of evil. "More tortuous than all else is the human heart, beyond remedy; who can understand it?" (Jer. 17:9). Human sinfulness appears almost as a "second nature" and is an impediment to the wholesome development of the religious, moral, and social life.

This idea of the pervasiveness of sin is associated with a deep sense of solidarity among human beings. Individualism of the sort that was to develop much later in Western thought is not present in the Hebrew Scriptures. The individual is, indeed, an individual, but each individual is intimately related to others in a common destiny both in good and in evil. This sense of solidarity is reflected at two levels: solidarity among contemporaries, and solidarity among successive generations. At the first level, solidarity is expressed in the conviction that the sin of one or of a minority may affect the whole of the nation. At the second level, solidarity is found in the conviction that children must bear the effects of the sins of their parents. Concepts in which this sense of solidarity is expressed, such as corporate personality, are based not on some sort of juridical fiction but on the concrete experience that the lives of human persons are inextricably intertwined. No one's possibilities before God are isolated from the situation in which the individual exists concretely.

The sense of solidarity among successive generations may be clarified further in the concept of a history of sin. This is clearly expressed in Genesis if we read at least to the eleventh chapter. Then it becomes clear that once sin has become a part of human history, it reaches out further and further like the rings of water when we drop a stone into a still pool. So pervasive does sin become that "[the Lord] regretted that he had made [humankind] on the earth, and his heart was grieved" (Gn. 6:6). The generations from Adam to Noah culminate in the destruction of sinful humanity and the rebirth of the world from the waters of the Flood. Again, the covenant with Noah is followed by the table of the nations culminating in the story of the tower of Babel. Sin is a power of evil at work in the history of the human race from the start, and it reaches out in every direction to touch all.

When the Genesis story of the Fall is read with these factors in mind, it becomes understandable that recent exegesis is strongly inclined to see this as a form of etiological narrative. This designation points to the conviction that the basic intent of the story is not to describe particular events at the beginning of human history, but to describe the causes of the sinful and painful history of humanity. As far as the intention of the writer is concerned, it is relatively unimportant whether the narrative is an account of particular historical facts. Rahner adds the qualification *historical* to the term *etiology* to express his conviction that while we are dealing with a literary device, the story does include some level of fact.[2] Hulsbosch carries the notion of etiology further and concludes that there is no specific historical fact that serves as the basis of the story.[3] In either of these views of etiology, it becomes unnecessary to think of original justice or the paradisial condition as an actual description of what humanity was like at some time in the past.

Thus, if one were to isolate the facts that constitute the concern of Genesis, they will be facts of a theological nature that are inaccessible to the sciences as such. The first and most basic fact is that of creation; all that exists comes from the power of a loving, beneficent God. Added to this is that the Creator calls human beings together with the cosmos to the fullness of life that can flow from an intimate relation of covenant partnership with God. The concrete human situation, however, is marked by the reality that human beings have failed and continue to fail in their response to God. Yet God does not give up. God is faithful to the divine promise. The power of goodness and love will eventually overcome the power of evil and sin. Thus, the account of the beginnings can be compared to the overture of an opera. In a Wagnerian overture, each leitmotiv introduces the audience to a character, an object, or a theme that will appear during the opera. Similarly, the opening chapters of Genesis introduce the reader to the characters and the dynamics of what will follow in the history of sin and salvation.

The significance of this as historical etiology consists in the fact that the sinful condition of the human race is to be traced not to ontological structures of being, nor to some prehistorical conflict between primal principles of good and evil, but rather precisely within history and at least in part to the way human agents have responded to God.[4] Adopting a fully mythical understanding of

---

2 *Hominisation*, pp. 36–44.
3 *God's Creation*, pp. 51–57.

the Fall, P. Ricoeur summarizes the significance of the account as follows:

> The fall is a cæsura cutting across everything that makes man human; everything—sexuality and death, work and civilization, culture and ethics—depends on both a primordial nature, lost but yet still lying there underneath, and an evil which although radical, is nonetheless contingent.[5]

Summarizing the point that the etiological interpretation underscores, Ricoeur writes: "The myth proclaims the purely 'historical' character of radical evil; it prevents it from being regarded as primordial evil."[6]

Thus, whether one adopts the pure etiology of Hulsbosch, the historical etiology of Rahner, or the fully mythical position of Ricoeur, the common implication is that it becomes less important to have any concrete image of the biological origins of the human race. What is at stake theologically is the universal human condition of sin for which humanity is, at least in part, responsible through the faulty exercise of human freedom. Because of the way we have exercised our accountability in and for history, we are alienated from our God-intended destiny and hence from our own deepest identity and from the world around us. The exegete and the theologian are not con-strained to say that at one time, the world was really different from the way it is now. Rather, they are inclined to say that if humanity had not intervened in the course of history by a disordered turning to self, our experience of ourselves and our world would be different. That we experience reality as we do today is the result of sin—that of earlier ages and that of today.

It is clear that independently of any question raised by evo-lutionary thought, the current readings of Genesis represent not a theological loss but a remarkable gain in the richness of the theology of sin that has emerged. It is clear, furthermore, that whether one continues to talk of an individual first sin of an individual human being, it is not the intent of Genesis to attribute all of our painful experience to that one sin alone, but to the first sin taken together

---

4   K. Rahner, *Theological Investigations I*, "Theological Reflections on Monogenism" (London, 1961) pp. 229–296.

5   *The Symbolism of Evil* (Boston, 1967, 1969 pbk) p. 250.

6   Ibid., p. 251.

with the entire history of sinfulness that flows from it. If, with Rahner, one chooses to speak of a first sin, the special significance of that first sinful action lies not in that it alone causes our present condition, but in that it truly initiates human sinfulness. Sins of succeeding generations will deepen the reality and the power of sin, but the *original* sin keeps its unique significance as the irreversible origin of sinfulness.

Romans 5

If the modern reading of the Hebrew Scriptures opens the way to a richer theological understanding of sin, the same can be said of the text of Romans, chapter 5. The older interpretation of Paul that takes him to speak of Adam simply as an individual human person through whose personal sin all others become sinners and are subject to death is based, to a great extent, on a faulty translation from the Greek to the Latin. Once this translation has been corrected, it becomes less clear that the text requires us to envision one sinner at the beginning of history from whose sin all of us become sinners. Rather, Paul is speaking of the first sin in as far as it is connected with all the sins of other human beings. The first sin has unleashed the power of sin in the world, a power that works itself out in the personal sins of all other human beings. As in the Hebrew Scriptures, so also with Paul there is a deep sense of human solidarity in the history of human sinfulness. The solidarity of the race brings with it not only suffering but a real state of sinful separation from God.

The object of Paul's teaching is not the biological descent of all humans from Adam, nor some primordial state of grace. Positively, Paul's principal concern is to affirm our solidarity in the grace of Christ, who is the cause of redemption for all human beings. To show how the deed of one can be of positive significance for all, Paul reaches back to the Hebrew tradition where the law of solidarity seems to be most apparent. If justification through Christ is the best example of solidarity in the positive sense, the Genesis tradition is the clearest expression of solidarity in sin. Hence, the Adam-Christ parallel. From Adam springs the old human race, penetrated through and through by the powers of sin and death. From Christ springs a new race, reborn in the power of the grace of Christ that opens to true life.

Thus, exegetes are inclined to hold that if Paul had any specific image of the biological origins of the human race, it is more than likely that he would have envisioned one man and one woman at the beginning. This, however, is not the point of his teaching, which is principally concerned with the grace of redemption in Christ, for which the universal sinful condition is the negative presupposition. Echoing the opinion of many exegetes, J. de Fraine concludes that Paul teaches nothing explicit about the strictly individual unicity of the first sinner.[7]

If we assess these two areas of biblical interpretation with reference to the question of monogenism or polygenism, we can conclude that monogenism is not directly taught nor necessarily implied by Scripture. What is at stake is above all the reality of human solidarity in sin. But in biblical terms, there can be a genuine solidarity that does not necessarily appeal to a biological basis. Paul himself writes in the same epistle in which he has spoken of Adam: "For not all who are of Israel are Israel, nor are they all children of Abraham because they are his descendants" (Rm. 9:6–7). Both Genesis and Romans can be understood legitimately to speak of Adam by way of a literary device. The monogenistic style of speech is the means of proposing the doctrine rather than the content of the doctrine itself.

Trent

Over and above the texts of Genesis and Romans, Catholic theology must take into account the teaching of the Council of Trent concerning the doctrine of original sin. The teaching of this council is not only a clear statement of an ecumenical council but is also the point at which the formulations of earlier synods and provincial councils come together. In this sense, it can be seen as a summary of the development of the doctrine of original sin at the official level of the Church.

Just as with Scripture, so also here, the way one approaches the texts is crucial to the outcome. As the Church, through a number of papal encyclicals, has encouraged the prudent use of historical-critical methodology in biblical studies, so also the Sacred Congregation for the Doctrine of the Faith has made a helpful statement on the use

---

7 *The Bible and the Origin of Man*, p. 60.

of similar methods in reading the later documents of the theological tradition.[8] In this statement, the congregation presents some helpful guidelines for approaching such documents as those of Trent, thereby lending official encouragement to methods that had been used by theologians for some time before this statement. In encouraging the use of historical-critical methods, however, the congregation does not thereby condone any particular result that theologians claim to derive by the use of these methods.

Of great significance for our reflections here is the distinction that this document makes between the meaning of dogmatic formulas, which remain ever true and constant, and the actual linguistic formulation itself. Furthermore, it speaks of the difficulty of interpreting the formulas correctly. And given the possibility of establishing the correct interpretation, it does not follow that a dogmatic formulation "has always been or will always be" suitable for communicating the truth of the faith to the same extent. Finally, it is one of the tasks of theologians to aid the Magisterium in determining the proper interpretation. In brief, the congregation recognizes that dogmatic formulas are created in historical situations; they are culturally conditioned and limited in their usefulness. It is conceivable that the same truth expressed in a particular formula could be expressed in quite different terms. The task of theology is not simply to repeat ancient formulas in a blind way, but to seek the genuine theological content and attempt to find a more adequate means of expressing this in relation to the total body of Church teaching and in relation to changing experiences of the Christian people in their particular cultural situations.

As regards the teaching of Trent in particular, the formulations that bear on the question of original sin reflect certain assumptions that may legitimately be distinguished from the theological issue at stake. The acts of the council itself make it sufficiently clear that the principal concern of Trent was not the doctrine of sin as much as it was the theology of justification, for this had become problematic because of the positions of Luther and other Protestant leaders of the time. What is found in the documents of Trent concerning the issue of

---

8 *Mysterium Ecclesiae: Declaration in Defense of the Catholic Doctrine on the Church against Certain Errors of the Present Day* (June 24, 1973). Available from United States Catholic Conference, Washington, DC.

sin must be seen as a function of the positive theology of justification in Christ. This can be qualified further as an attempt to cut a middle way between the naturalistic humanism of the Renaissance and the somewhat pessimistic theology of extrinsic justification coming from the Protestant leaders. The question at stake is the question as to how deeply justification and grace reach into human life. The Tridentine teaching is an attempt to uphold the traditional Scholastic view that saw God's grace as a power that reaches deeply into the core of the human person to transform it from within. Grace does not sit on the surface of human life. On the other hand, grace cannot be simply identified with human nature. Thus, Scholastic theology, making use of Aristotelian categories, could speak of grace as a supernatural habit that inheres in the soul. It is not simply identical to existing as a human being, but neither is it external to the human person. It is a mode of existing whereby, through the power of God's presence, the human person is transformed from the deepest recesses of his or her personal being.

If this is the case with justification, the understanding of sin must parallel this. If grace is not on the surface of life, neither is sin. The reality of sin touches human life as deeply as grace. Furthermore, if all human beings stand in need of the positive influence of God's grace in Christ, it must follow that all are involved in a sinful situation that embraces all and that conditions each human person interiorly at the personal core of existence. Thus, each human being—from the very beginning of life—stands in factual contradiction to the saving will of God, who has created all things with a view to Christ, and who wills to bring creation to fulfillment in Christ. The teaching of Trent, therefore, is an attempt to say that the salvation that God desires for each of us is not factually communicated to us together with our origins as human persons. Therefore, a contradiction exists between our relation to Christ and our actual historical condition whereby we stand in the universal solidarity of sinfulness. In line with the tradition that bases itself on Genesis, Trent associates the factual sinfulness of our situation with free, historical actions of human beings.

Thus, as a condition for Trent's doctrine on justification, the council presents its teaching on the universal sinful state of the human race. Following the principles of the historical-critical method, we can distinguish this theological issue from the actual verbal formulations of Trent; indeed, our own statement above has made minimal use of Tridentine language. To interpret any text presumes that the interpreter can say the same thing in at least two different ways. But a further distinction is suggested by a number of authors who follow the lead of Schoonenberg in this regard. Schoonenberg argues that we must distinguish between the intention of the conciliar fathers and the presuppositions they may have had because of their historical situation. He argues further that some presuppositions may be necessary for the truth of the principal statement, while others may not be necessary even though their presence in the mind of the author clearly shapes his language.[9]

With regard to Trent, if one were to press the Church fathers as to their concrete image of the beginnings of history, they would, without doubt, have seen it in terms of what we today call biological monogenism. This presupposition clearly has left its mark on the language of the council, which speaks unabashedly as though there were an individual man named Adam at the beginning of human history. But it is legitimate to ask whether this presupposition is necessarily connected with the theological teaching on justification and on sin.[10] It seems a responsible position to hold that the presupposition of the Fathers is not strictly necessary for their doctrine of the universality of sin, though those who hold such a position have the task of providing a convincing alternative that can explain the universality of sin as well or perhaps even better.

A final point of interest may be seen in the careful formulation of *Humani generis*, to which we have already referred. Given the situation in 1950, Pope Pius XII was in a position to give a clear interpretation of the Tridentine text. Yet he did not point to the teaching of Trent as clear evidence against polygenism; nor did he define the numerical unicity of Adam. On the other hand, he clearly pointed to the theological problem that was connected with such a theory—namely, the universality of sin. It is possible to see the position of Pius XII as an official interpretation of the teaching of Trent, an interpretation that does not close the possibility that theology may be able to account for

---

9 *Man and Sin*, p. 51.

10 Ibid., p. 169.

the tradition's concern for universality on some basis other than the biological theory of monogenism.

We must point out also that the teaching of Trent is not completely identical with the teaching of the commonly used catechetical materials that have informed the Christian consciousness of generations of American Catholics, such as the Baltimore Catechism. Not all that appears in the Baltimore Catechism is to be found in Trent. In particular, the description of a state of paradisial existence is significantly absent from Trent. In deference to positions disputed in Scholastic theology, the Fathers of Trent made a rather cautious statement on the grace of the first man without resolving the question in dispute between the schools. This, together with a limited statement on the relation between sin and concupiscence and sin and death, is about all that remains of the traditional doctrine of the supernatural and preternatural gifts of Paradise in the text of Trent.

Keeping in mind the distinction between intent and verbal formulation, and that between presuppositions and direct statements, we can restate the intended meaning of Trent in the following way. Explicitly excluding the Blessed Virgin from its statement, the council intends to say that every human person is interiorly affected in the moral-religious sphere of personal existence by the mere fact of being born into the human community. This is to be seen as a real alienation from God, yet it is not to be confused with personal sin. It involves no structural change in the nature of the human person, but is understood to affect the unity of nature and grace in such a way that the human person does not have full personal possession of its nature. This situation affects all human relations in the world, including our final experience in history, the experience of death. Experiencing the world in a sinful condition is different from experiencing the world without sin.

Understood in this way, the Church's doctrine on sin can be seen in contrast with dualism and idealism. Dualism tends to explain the brokenness of the world by tracing evil back to a metaphysical principle of evil, thus turning finite reality into an ultimate power. Idealism, on the other hand, by overemphasizing the harmony of all reality, tends to minimize the significance of sin. The Church's doctrine refuses to take either of these alternatives. Unlike dualism, it does not see evil as an ultimate principle. Unlike idealism, it takes the reality of sin with great seriousness, locating its roots in the free, historical acts of human beings. Thus, it attempts to take human responsibility seriously without minimizing the reality of sin and without turning it into a metaphysical principle.

Major Shifts in Perspective

We are now in a position to describe the major changes in outlook among theologians concerning the theology of original sin. In general terms, the most creative attempts to restate the understanding of sin do so with an eye to evolutionary thought and make a switch from the more "essentialist" style of Scholastic theology to one that is more "personalist." Thinking in terms of evolutionary categories, these theologians tend to interpret the biblical theology of creation as related to the historical, evolutionary process. In brief, God creates toward an end or purpose. What comes forth from the creative action of God is not a finished reality, but an unfinished world that is being led by God to the end that God has in mind for it. This general orientation takes on a specifically Christian coloration from the theology of resurrection, which allows theologians to say that the end is anticipated in Christ. In view of the mystery of Christ's glorification, we come to know something of what God intends for the world. And from the same point of reference, we come to know something about what stands in the way of the world moving to that end; this is the question of sin.

One of the basic elements of the new formulations now emerges. Sin, from the beginning, is to be understood in terms of creation's relation to Christ. If Christ is the revelation of the end as well as the way to the end, then sin is always a deviation from the way that Christ reveals. If the end and the way revealed in Christ have always been the end and the way to which God calls the human race, then sin always is a deviation from that end and way, whether the sinner has been explicitly confronted with Christ or not. To say that original sin is a deviation from the way of Christ does not imply that the first human beings had some explicit knowledge of Christ. It means merely that as soon as sin entered into human history, the flow of history was diverted from the end that God had intended for it.

From the perspective of the future of the world as revealed in Christ, a second element common to the new formulations appears. This consists in the tendency to measure the "guilty lack" with which sin is concerned not in terms of a "lost possession," but in terms of the failure to move toward the only future that God intends for us. Grace is not something we once possessed and then lost. On the contrary, it is a gift to which God has called us throughout history, but our response, if not always totally negative, has been halting and limited.

Within this general orientation, we can distinguish some more radical solutions and some that are moderate in tone. The more radical positions either set aside the notion of the historical fact of a first sin (Hulsbosch), or tend to identify in various degrees the sin of Adam with the sin of humanity in general (Schoonenberg and Trooster). The view of Schoonenberg depends largely on sociological categories to explain original sin as a *situation* into which each individual is born. This situation is seen to involve the practical inevitability of sinning personally because of the weight of evil present in the situation. Such a position has the advantage of expressing something that is experienced in concrete terms by many in modern society—namely, the oppressive and limiting character of the human situation into which they are born.

Less radical than this are attempts such as those of Alszeghy-Flick. Their work represents a sustained effort to present a personalist concept of sin within an evolutionary worldview. In essence, sin is the incapacity to dialogue that infects all human beings born into this world, reaching both to the horizontal level of dialogue with fellow humans and to the vertical level of dialogue with God. This incapacity for dialogue is sinful not merely because human persons are born into a sinful situation and will inevitably commit sin themselves, but because before any personal, moral decision of their own, they "belong to the world," which has rejected God's invitation. This seems to be an elaboration of the notion of corporate personality, and therein lies some of the difficulty with this position. It is not clear precisely what the metaphysical implications of this concept might be, and it is not fully adequate simply to offer a historical description of the concept as operative in Scripture.

Whatever other problems may be contained in this opinion, it is clear that Alszeghy-Flick do not deny a first sin. For them, there is a first sin, but there is together with this the accumulation of all the sins committed by all individuals and by society subsequent to that first sin. This latter component of their view is called the "sin of the world." Thus, without denying the reality of a first sin, they succeed in showing that it is not that one sin alone that causes the sinful condition for people of later generations. The first sin has unleashed a power of sin in history. Both the first and all subsequent sins constitute the situation into which the individual is born. Though no individual is personally culpable except when she or he personally sins, each is born into an environment that is oriented in the wrong direction. It is a world that is insensitive to God and resists the divine call. Thus, even the child, while having no personal culpability, is in the full sense of the word a member of a community that, through the culpable actions of its members, has constituted itself historically in opposition to God.

Positions such as these may be evaluated in terms of two types of questions: (1) Are they valid supplements to the traditional sort of statement concerning sin? (2) Are they adequate statements of the traditional concern? In reply to the first sort of question it may be said that both approaches do present valid concerns of the biblical tradition as well as of the later tradition that are frequently left out of the common presentation of sin. Ordinary catechesis tends to isolate the issue of the one sin at the beginning of history and the resultant sinful condition of each individual in subsequent generations without saying anything concerning the historical mediation of sin through human relations and social and economic structures. In this regard, such presentations are inadequate and need to be supplemented by the valid insights that can be gained from the work of Schoonenberg, Alszeghy-Flick, and others. Not only will the doctrine of original sin gain in convincing power for Christian believers, but it will be more faithful to the fuller biblical and theological tradition.

The second sort of question concerning the adequacy of the newer presentations is not as easy to answer. In both cases, whether they are able to give an adequate statement of the traditional concern for the depth with which sin affects the human person will depend on a more adequate philosophy of relation. Sin is here described principally in terms of relation, and since relation is commonly conceived in classical theology as one of the categories of accidental being, many are convinced that what is said in such theories, while good in itself, is simply not enough. On the other hand, those who would be inclined to give more metaphysical weight to the reality of relations, as is done in process philosophy, would likewise be inclined to say that relation is not peripheral to our concrete being, but enters deeply into the core of our personal identity. If this is the case, it is conceivable that the attempt to elaborate a fuller understanding of relation could lead to greater acceptability for such positions.

– 6 –

THE NEW CREATION:
Creation and Eschatology

The Future of God's Creation

One of the factors in creation theology that has arisen from scriptural studies is the connection between creation and eschatology. For those of us who have been accustomed to think of eschatology as a tract discussed at the end of any systematic theology, this may come as a surprise. It may likewise be surprising to discover that eschatology is something more than the discussion of the "last things"—death, judgment, heaven, and hell.

Eschatology is central to the biblical experience of God and the divine promise. This is true for both the Hebrew Scriptures and the Christian Scriptures, and it provides one of the connecting links between the history of Jesus and the Jewish traditions to which he was heir. This fact is of far-reaching significance for theology because it means that eventually eschatology must help shape the fundamental theological categories in all the tracts of systematic theology. We will limit our remarks to a discussion of the relation between creation and eschatology.

Already in discussing the Scriptures with regard to the general doctrine of creation, we see eschatological language emerging. We also can reverse that observation to say that in speaking of eschatology, the Scriptures frequently speak the language of creation. If, as Schillebeeckx argues, the God experience of the Jewish tradition is centered in the experience of promise,[1] and if the fully developed language in which the fulfillment of promise is expressed is eschatological language, then the conjunction of creation language and eschatological language can designate the fulfillment of that which God originates in creating. In terms of one stream of the Hebrew tradition, eschatological language speaks of God's ultimate vindication of the divine act of creation. Hence, the question of eschatology eventually raises the question of the nature and meaning of the history in which God's creation unfolds.

The Heart of Christian Eschatology

In speaking of creation, we have seen above that our language becomes highly symbolic rather than flatly literal. When we recognize that the transposition of creation language into the mode of fulfillment constitutes one of the principal forms of eschatological language, we realize that in eschatology we are dealing with one of the most thoroughly symbolic forms of expression. The reason for this becomes apparent when we think of how it is that we speak about the future at all.

Eschatology is not simply futurology, but is a particular way of speaking of the future from the basis of a religious experience. Yet, since it is in some way talk about a future, the inner dynamic of it may be perceived already at those levels in which we speak of our future in an everyday sense of the word. Fundamentally we speak of the future from out of the experience of the present. In as far as present experience includes the polarities of good and evil, when we dream of a better future, we envision overcoming the evil factors in the present and maximizing the good in the present experience. We dream of a better tomorrow, or of the world as a better place in which to live. A similar dynamic may be perceived in the development of Christian eschatological language. The principal difference rests in that the present experience from which it proceeds is a religious experience; specifically, as Rahner has suggested, it is the present experience of God's grace in Christ.[2] Our present experience of the saving grace

---

1 E. Schillebeeckx, *God the Future of Man.* tr. N. D. Smith (London/Sydney, 1969) pp. 169–203.

2 "Eschatology" in *Sacramentum mundi* 2 (New York/London, 1968) pp. 242–246; "The Hermeneutics of Eschatological Assertions," in *Theological Investigations* 4 (London, 1966) pp. 323–346, esp. 332–333.

of God is already an eschatological mystery because the ultimate dimensions of meaning impinge on our present reality. Yet our present is still so mixed with evil, pain, and limitation that we are led to turn our gaze to the fulfillment of this present experience of grace. As Rahner argues, eschatology as a Christian mode of discourse is a projection of fulfillment from the present experience of the human situation in as far as the present is already conditioned by the mystery of the Christ event.

Viewed in this way, eschatology is not a fund of arcane information about events that are to take place at the end of history. Such a detailed reporting of future events is seen by Rahner as apocalyptic. Rather, the highly symbolic language of eschatology has as its purpose to hold open an awareness of a future that remains always obscure so that in light of the hoped-for future, believers may accept their present as a real factor in the actualization of the possibility that was initiated by God in creation. The relation between creation theology and eschatology might be expressed in the following way. Eschatology speaks of the fulfillment of what is initiated by God in creation. Viewed the other way around, creation is the placing of the possibility of the fulfillment. In as far as that fulfillment is realized in the Resurrection of Jesus Christ, Christian eschatology lives from this fundamental, positive statement: Jesus Christ really lives with God. In as far as the Resurrection of Jesus is the anticipation of the destiny of the human race, Christian theology affirms the Christian conviction that we also have a future with God. And it is in the future that the mystery of our existence as created beings is ultimately vindicated. Eschatology points to the fulfilling completion of our being as creatures.

When eschatology is approached in this way, it is possible to distinguish between this fundamental eschatological awareness and an apocalyptic fascination with events of the end-times about which Jesus himself was so reserved.[3] Perhaps such matters will never cease to fascinate the human imagination, but the resolution of such apocalyptic questions does not pertain to the core of Christian faith. It is possible also to distinguish between the core issue and the many symbolic expressions in which this is called to our awareness. Such

---

3   Mt. 24:36 reserves knowledge of the last day to the heavenly Father alone.

symbols as the heavenly banquet, the Kingdom of God, and the heavenly Jerusalem each in its own way expresses something of that future without giving us specific information about it. Thus, Rahner can say that Christians are those who believe firmly that we have a future with God, but they know remarkably little about what it will be.

It would be beyond the scope of this book to take up the individual themes of eschatological symbolism. That would require another treatment in itself. It is sufficient for our purposes in reflecting on the theology of creation to see that there is an internal connection between creation and eschatology. From a Christian perspective, that which unifies them is the mystery of Christ. As God creates in and through the eternal Word, so God redeems and brings to ultimate completion through the Incarnation and glorification of the same Word embodied in Jesus of Nazareth. The Word embodied in Jesus is the medium in and through which God always reaches to the world, creating, transforming through grace, and perfecting in eschatological fulfillment. Creation, as the going forth from God, is simultaneously the first step of the return to God, and the return is the completion of the journey begun in creation. God creates for a purpose that becomes known as the future of the world in the Resurrection of Jesus, the Christ.

So it is that Christians have a passionate belief that humanity and the cosmos have a future. And the future is the completion of the incarnational order of creation whereby God becomes ever more at one with creation, and creation is transformed through the power of that loving, divine presence into the personal likeness of God in a history of spiritual growth through the exercise of human freedom.

The future of the world to which Christians look in hope is a future that even though it is worked out in history will find its ultimate fulfillment in a state that transcends our historical experience. It will be that final state of existence with God in which the creative power of God's self-giving love will totally suffuse all creaturely relations, transforming all into the final perfection of love and mutuality. And "God may be all in all" (1 Cor. 15:28).

- 7 -

Prospects

As we have indicated already, we need some sort of synthesis, even though many believe that the time is not yet ripe for that. Any attempted synthesis will, of necessity, be provisional. The question of synthesis again raises the question of the larger worldview that would be involved — that is, the relation between the theological concerns of creation, sin, and eschatology to the way we experience the world today. The question might be put in the following way. If an Augustine was able to speak theologically in a world conditioned by neo-Platonism, and if an Aquinas was able to construct a theology using Aristotelian categories to speak to a world wrestling with the Aristotelian worldview, is it possible for contemporary theology to do a similar thing for our times, taking a specifically contemporary worldview as a dialogue partner?

When the question is phrased in that way, the first issue is to determine what is meant by a contemporary worldview. At no level — whether in science or in philosophy — can we speak of a universally accepted worldview. Yet, at least in a provisional way, it does seem possible to single out some dominant characteristics that seem quite pervasive. Among these is certainly the emergence of historical consciousness. One need not espouse any form of biological evolution to recognize the common fact of our cultural experience that human beings today experience themselves in a world that seems in many ways quite unstable and incomplete. In such a world, they feel themselves as active agents in working on the world for good or for evil. In some ways that may be difficult to define exactly, the destiny of the physical world seems to be intimately linked with the destiny of the human race and hence with the many free, creative decisions made by human beings in history. It would be relatively easy to say that this feeling is exactly the experience of pride that has been so fatal in human history and is to be rejected by the Christian believer. The task of religion and theology would then be seen as waging the battle against such modernity.

Yet the mainline Western tradition has consistently resisted such a choice. It has more often than not recognized the need for a relation to culture that affirms the values to be found there even as it takes a critical stance with respect to the evils present in a given situation. The traditional style of the mainline Western theological tradition has been to search for a genuine contextual relevance whereby Christianity, while remaining true to its own deepest identity, can enrich human culture, and culture can enrich theology and the life of faith.

Fidelity to such a tradition leads one inevitably to ask about the possibilities of at least a hesitant and provisional attempt to speak of the fundamental theological issues in terms of the modern experience of historical consciousness. While recognizing that many particular questions still await more adequate treatment, we will close our reflections with some suggestions as to what the broader contours of such a synthesis might look like.

From the perspective of science, the emergence of the human race on earth seems to fit into an evolutionary view of this planet and of its immediate cosmic context. The most common elements formed from our sun seem to be taken up in a process that moves from simple forms to more complex forms. From nonliving forms, we move to living forms of great variety. As complexity increases, there is a corresponding increase in intelligence and self-consciousness. This "biological ascent" has been described by Teilhard as a process of complexification. Complexification increases gradually to certain critical points at which a qualitative difference emerges. Teilhard's vision of the history of the world looks much like the classical, vertical hierarchy of beings (nonliving, living, intelligent) now turned over into a horizontal position and seen as a hierarchy that is achieved through a temporal process of development. Moving from prelife forms, Teilhard speaks of geogenesis, biogenesis, and noogenesis.

The interpretation of the relation of simpler to more complex forms raises the question of value judgments immediately. Not hesitating to make such judgments, Teilhard interprets the data of paleontology, archeology, and so on, to mean that we are taken up in a process of evolution that finds its meaning in intelligent life. The significance of intelligent, self-conscious life is that evolution here becomes a self-directing process. But the basic movement of complexity consciousness does not stop when humanity appears.

Rather, the same law is operative in the social development of the human race. For Teilhard, evolution is a movement whereby created reality becomes more deeply personal and social through history.

We are not concerned with details of this description, nor with the fullest cosmic projection that Teilhard makes, but simply with the view that humanity is taken up in a historical process, and that this human, historical process is deeply embedded in the history of a constantly changing world. Whether we accept Teilhard's premise is not the question. The sense of historicity and of cosmic context is. The human race has a history as does each individual human person, and the quality of our human life is clearly intertwined with the physical world in which it is so deeply rooted. The principal question for theology is whether any significant light can be given to this sense of historicity from divine revelation.

Our earlier reflections on the source materials emphasized the theological conviction that God creates toward a goal, and Christians perceive something of that goal in Christ. We have seen also that the history of humanity is from the beginning conditioned by the realities of God's grace and human sin. Such theological data seem, in their own way, to imply a positive assessment of time and history. This helps to clarify why the Bible itself, to a great extent, is a theological reflection on history. It sheds further light on the fact that for centuries before the emergence of Aristotelianism, the theology of Christianity was commonly cast within a historical framework. And at a number of crucial points, the theology of history was taken up as a specific concern. This is the case with Augustine, Honorius of Autun, Rupert of Deutz, Joachim of Fiore, and Bonaventure. For these earlier theologies of history, the physical world appears as the stage on which the history of humanity is acted out. The question for us is whether the physical world is such a stable stage, or whether it too in some way is involved in the process of history. The issue is not whether evolution proves faith, or whether faith proves evolution. Rather, it is a question of recognizing first that there is no incompatibility between the religious experience of a Christ-centered history of creation, which finds its completion in eschatological fulfillment, and the modern sense of the historicity of the world and of humanity. Both seem to imply an experience of the fundamental incompleteness of created reality as we now find it, together with an openness to a level of completion that does not now exist. In principle, the Christian religious experience and the modern experience of historicity are not opposed to each other.

May we go beyond this statement of noncontradiction? Is it possible to see a more positive relation between the two? It was Teilhard's conviction that it is possible, and in a limited way, we share that conviction. For Teilhard, an explicit connection is made between the evolutionary world of science and the Christ-centered world of faith in as far as the last stage of human evolution (the social convergence of the human community) is identified with the convergence of the world on its final point, Christ Omega. What appears to the sciences as a process of cosmogenesis is seen from the perspective of faith to be a process of Christogenesis. As the true meaning of a process is seen in the fruit that it produces, so the world process is seen in its true meaning only in the full mystery of Christ: Jesus Christ together with the community of human love gathered around him in the presence of God. Without Christ, the evolutionary process remains fundamentally unintelligible.

Such a contact between science and faith, though it raises many problems that are not fully resolved by Teilhard, can appeal to clear precedents in the cosmic Christology of Paul and the Word Christology of John, as well as in the Logos speculation of the Apologists, the great patristic writers such as Athanasius and Maximus Confessor, and the medieval Franciscan tradition as represented by Bonaventure and Scotus.

While theology depends on science for information on the concrete flow of evolutionary history, science as such can provide no framework for interpreting the ultimate levels of meaning. This is the proper task of theology. The incomplete world of evolution-ary thought can be given a faith-inspired interpretation that would have for modern believers the same significance that the synthesis of Aquinas had for believers of the thirteenth century.

God creates toward an end. That end as embodied in Christ points to a Christified world. What appears from one viewpoint as a process of biological evolution and cultural history may be seen from another viewpoint as a history of the creative self-communication of God in ongoing interaction with the world and humanity. The biblical history reflects the growing religious awareness of the deeper levels of meaning in what otherwise might appear as a process devoid of final significance. History is a divine epiphany through which the world and humanity is brought to completion.

It is through this history of revelation that Christians come to perceive that the ground or source of the creative process is a limit-less mystery of productive love. The creative ground is fruitful love; the mystery of the divine is the love community in itself. This is but another way of saying that God is triune. This being the case, it should not be surprising to see that the entire process of history reflects the mystery of fruitful love in a variety of analogous ways. Science sees a process whereby, as in basic chemical elements, individual elements unite with each other to form something new, as hydrogen and oxygen unite to become water. One would hesitate to call this love, but it is possible to see a certain distant analogy with the experience of human love. Isolated, independent existence must be given up to enter into broader and potentially deeper levels of existence.

It is when humanity enters the scene that this principle of unification for the sake of fuller existence takes on truly personal dimensions and is seen as love in the proper sense of the word. God's creative love freely calls forth within the world a created love that can freely respond to God's creative call. The process of evolution has a direction or goal. But the process is not a mechanistic one. With the emergence of humanity, it is fraught with ambiguity and with the danger of frustration. God risks creating a creature that has the capability of building its history in conflict with the intent of God.

The human race, it seems, emerges in a harsh and painful world, a world that operates on the basis of principles other than that of love—principles such as competition, cleverness, and strength. To say that God is love and that God creates out of love is not to say that God creates a perfect world or a best possible world. Nor is it to say that in the beginning all things existed in a state of paradisial peace and harmony. It is to say, however, that in as far as God creates a good world, it is a world that is fit for the working out of the divine purpose. If this purpose is directed to the ever-widening expansion of created persons in loving union among themselves and with God, then it is significant to ask not whether God could have created a different sort of world, but whether the divine purpose may be realized in this actual world. The insight of Irenæus of Lyons is suggestive here. He held that the history of the world was a movement from imperfection to greater perfection, from immaturity to greater maturity, so that humanity might learn to bear the mystery of its loving God and thus come to fullness of life. We are created in a world that from the beginning needs to grow. Since the passage from immaturity to maturity requires some form of challenge, God has created us in a world full of challenges.

What Irenæus saw as the childhood of the human race we may see as the primitive quality of the first human beings—profoundly rooted in the earth, yet with an exalted future before them, a future of which they could have no inkling as they turned to the rough and primitive world surrounding them and struggled for survival. From the start, human nature has labored under a deficiency that is clearly physical in nature. But physical deficiency and evolutionary incompleteness is not yet sin.

It is possible to speak of sin only when those primitive beginnings are seen in relation to the goal to which God is calling creation. Understandable and inevitable as the struggle for survival is, when it is viewed from the perspective of the ideal embodied in Christ, the law of survival cannot be other than ultimately self-destructive if it is accepted as an adequate basis for human relations and human ethics. Judged from the perspective of Christian agapistic love, humanity emerges in evolutionary history in a way that—in the short view—is inevitable for mere survival, but which—in the long view—can become self-destructive; for it will make it difficult to allow that quality of life to emerge in which human fulfillment ultimately resides.

The physical deficiency and evolutionary incompleteness of humanity in its early stages are themselves factors in the moral deficiency that comes to infest human history. Humanity embarks upon its journey in a way that amounts to a rejection of the future that God intends for it. As that self-destructive response becomes structured in social and cultural forms, it is solidified and strengthened and mediated to ongoing generations, creating the stubborn rigidities in the world that stand in the way of the realization of God's intention. Sin is experienced as closedness, an inability to love, and a disordering from that quality of life in loving communion with others and with God to which the evolutionary history is being called by God.

Thus, human history—conceived in Christian terms—is from the beginning a history of grace and sin. It is a history of grace, because the action of God always precedes the action of the creature. From the beginning and throughout the whole of history, God is calling creation to loving union with the divine mystery itself. What is significant is not that we exist as creatures, but that we exist as an open-ended possibility. We exist as the possibility of a deeper, richer quality of life that must be accomplished through our response to the world and to God. We exist as creatures whose earthiness can be transformed into Godlike life. We exist as creatures whose existence can be deepened and enriched by personal union with the God who is the source of our being. This is to say that we exist as a potential for grace. Grace is not an option that we can reject and yet achieve authentic humanity. Our nature exists principally as the potential for a depth of life and love to be realized in union with God to some degree already within history, but ultimately in eschatological fulfillment. God's creative call lures us toward that end from the beginning of history.

Human history is a history of response, both negative and positive, to the lure of God's love. The negative response is the history of the human failure in moving toward that transformation that is our God-intended future. Sin is not a mere infringement of a law extrinsic to our nature. It is a failure to realize the potential of our nature itself. If our nature is fundamentally a potential to expand, sin is a contraction. If the history of evolution up to the emergence of humanity appears as a relatively consistent line of complexification and increased consciousness, with sin a reverse force has entered history. Sin is the resistance to expansion through union with others.

It is the attempt to create human history in alienation from the only end that we ultimately have. With sin, in the history of society eventually come all the structural rigidities that create and mediate the human world to oncoming generations and become real impediments to the development of the style of life embodied in Christ's agapistic love and symbolized in the metaphor of the Kingdom of God. Sin is a failure in the collaborative effort to move toward full personalization in human community.

If sin is the history of the negative response to God leading to alienation, separation, and isolation, the positive response is the history of grace leading to ever deeper union among human beings and of humanity with God. Though not restricted to Jews and Christians, the history of God's grace and human response finds a distinctive form of self-consciousness in the history of the Bible, and an unsurpassed level of realization in the person and destiny of Jesus Christ. As God's most personal Word to creation, Christ is the irrevocable call to community, to a universal community that transcends the limited communities based on bonds of blood, nation, or race. As the embodiment of what God intends for creation, Christ is simultaneously the criterion by which all deficiencies and sin can be recognized.

In earlier ages, Christians saw Christ as the end of the ages, and expected the immediate end of history. As centuries of Christian history passed, medieval theologians began to speculate that the "fullness of time" might coincide not with the end of time but with the center of time. In view of our present awareness of the extent of cosmic history and of the brief moment that makes up human history in that context, we might be inclined to see the coming of Christ not at the end nor at the center, but remarkably close to the beginning of human history.

The polarities of sin and grace remain throughout history, but the destiny of humanity has achieved a unique level of self-awareness in the consciousness of the Christian community. It remains forever the mission of that community to realize a certain quality of life in her members, to celebrate the levels of community that have been realized, and to invite others to share in what Christians see as God's dream for humanity. It is the dream of a universal community in which human beings will be reconciled among themselves and with the world in as far as they are reconciled with their God. God, who is love community, calls forth love community in creation through the free response of human persons to the offer of divine grace.

And the degree of reconciliation realized within history is the condition for that final communion between God and creation. That future, which lies beyond the limits of space-time experience, is the fruit of the interaction between God's free offer of grace and the free response of creatures. It is the full personalization of creation, which is realized in as far as human beings enter personally into the mystery of the divine Word, who has become incarnate in Jesus Christ, and by sharing in the personal mystery of the Word, enter into the Word's relation to the Father and the Spirit. The eschatological Omega point toward which creation is being drawn through history has been expressed nowhere with greater symbolic power than in the words of the thirteenth-century theologian, Bonaventure:

> Eternal life consists in this alone, that the rational spirit, which emanates from the most blessed trinity and is a likeness of the trinity, should return after the manner of an intelligible circle . . . to the most blessed trinity by God-conforming glory.[1]

Theology need not fear science nor tremble before the power of reason. Rather both theology and science need to stand in awe in the face of the mystery that is our world and in the even greater mystery of God to which the world points. We may well be astonished and overwhelmed by the immensity of the universe as seen through the eyes of science. It may be difficult to imagine that an intelligent God would act in such an extravagant and uneconomical manner. If the stellar systems were intended only to produce a planet capable of life, would an intelligent God have employed such vast machinery for this purpose?

We have no reason to assume that the mere fact of human life is the goal of the universe. What is important above all is a quality of life, not the mere fact of life. With this in mind, we can see that it is a more significant question to ask whether this sort of world is apt for the accomplishment of God's purpose. It is, indeed, a cosmos that challenges humanity in mind and in will, and that is capable of

---

1 *Quæstiones disputatæ de mysterio trinitatis*, q. 8, reply 7.

eliciting both awe and wonder. It is a cosmos that draws humanity out of the narrow point from which it begins to expand to the mystery of the world and thus to move toward the Ground of the world. It is a world apt to stretch the finite spirit to the limits of its possibility to bring forth not only the fact of life, but a Godlike quality of life that is a created sharing in the loving thought of God from which the whole of creation emerges.

Immensely complex in its present form, the cosmos is built of elements that are relatively few and simple. As both simple and complex, it reflects the mystery of God who, though supremely simple, is yet the boundlessly fertile source of the myriad forms of beings that constitute our universe. God the Creator appears not as an economist who must be sparing in the work of creation because of the meager resources available for creation. On the contrary, God appears as an artist whose concerns transcend the values of economy and pragmatism and whose signature is a beauty that is both tender and awesome. God the Creator is the divine artist who brings forth a world that is fit to open the human spirit to beauty, goodness, and love—in short, to values that move beyond everyday usefulness. And for the eye of faith, the world which God is even now fashioning is truly a window to the divine.

The cosmos as seen through the lense of modern science need not be a threat to belief in God. But such a vision of the world does, indeed, confront us with a question of great importance. How big a God do we believe in? It certainly gives reason to reflect on the fecundity and the creative artistry of the Creator.

Selected Bibliography

Creation

Brueggemann, W. *In Man We Trust: The Neglected Side of Biblical Faith*. Richmond, VA: John Knox Press, 1972.

Edwards, D. *Jesus and the Cosmos*. Mahwah, NJ: Paulist Press, 1991.

Gilkey, L. *Maker of Heaven and Earth: The Christian Doctrine of Creation in the Light of Modern Knowledge*. Garden City, NY: Doubleday, 1965 (Pbk).

Haught, J. *The Promise of Nature: Ecology and Cosmic Promise*. Mahwah, NJ: Paulist Press, 1993.

————. *Science and Religion: From Conflict to Conversation*. Mahwah, NJ: Paulist Press, 1995.

Hulsbosch, A. *God's Creation: Creation, Sin and Redemption in an Evolving World*. Tr. M. Versfeld. London, Melbourne, New York: Sheed & Ward, 1965 (Pbk).

Pendergast, R. *Cosmos*. New York: Fordham University Press, 1973.

Renckens, H. *Israel's Concept of the Beginning: The Theology of Genesis 1–3*. Tr. C. Naper. New York: Herder and Herder, 1964.

Scheffczyk, L. *Creation and Providence*. Tr. R. Strachan. London: Burns & Oates; New York: Herder and Herder, 1970.

Sin

Duffy, S. "Our Hearts of Darkness: Original Sin Revisited," in *Theological Studies* 49 (1988): 59–622.

Ricoeur, P. *Symbolism of Evil*. Tr. B. Buchanan. New York: Beacon Press, 1967. (Pbk).

Schoonenberg, P. *Man and Sin: A Theological View*. Tr. J. Donceel. South Bend, IN: University of Notre Dame Press, 1965.

Suchocki, M. H. *The Fall to Violence: Original Sin in Relational Theology*. New York: Continuum, 1994.

Trooster, S. *Evolution and the Doctrine of Original Sin.* Tr. J. A. Ter Haar. Glen Rock, NJ: Newman Press, 1968.

Eschatology

Hayes, Z. *Visions of a Future: A Study of Christian Eschatology.* Michael Glazier/ Liturgical Press, 1989.

Macquarrie, J. *Christian Hope.* New York: Seabury Press, 1978.

Rahner, K. "The Hermeneutics of Eschatological Assertions," in *Theological Investigations* 4. London: Darton, Longman, & Todd, 1966, pp. 323–346.

Ratzinger, J. Cardinal. *Eschatology: Death and Eternal Life.* Tr. M. Waldstein. Washington, DC: Catholic University Press, 1988.

Index